The New York Times

IN THE HEADLINES

Plastic

CAN THE DAMAGE BE REPAIRED?

THE NEW YORK TIMES EDITORIAL STAFF

**Published in 2020 by New York Times Educational Publishing
in association with The Rosen Publishing Group, Inc.
29 East 21st Street, New York, NY 10010**

First Edition

The New York Times
Caroline Que: Editorial Director, Book Development
Phyllis Collazo: Photo Rights/Permissions Editor
Heidi Giovine: Administrative Manager

Rosen Publishing
Megan Kellerman: Managing Editor
Hanna Washburn: Editor
Greg Tucker: Creative Director
Brian Garvey: Art Director

Cataloging-in-Publication Data
Names: New York Times Company.
Title: Plastic: can the damage be repaired? / edited by the New
York Times editorial staff.
Description: New York : The New York Times Educational Publish-
ing, 2020. | Series: In the headlines | Includes glossary and index.
Identifiers: ISBN 9781642823660 (library bound) | ISBN
9781642823653 (pbk.) | ISBN 9781642823677 (ebook)
Subjects: LCSH: Plastics—Environmental aspects. | Plastic scrap—
Environmental aspects. | Refuse and refuse disposal—Environmental
aspects. | Recycling (Waste, etc.)—Environmental aspects.
Classification: LCC TD798.P537 2020 | DDC 628.4'4—dc23

Manufactured in the United States of America

On the cover: An assortment of debris, largely plastic and
believed to be mostly from Indonesia, that has washed up on
the shores of Bremmer Island, off the coast of northern Australia,
July 3, 2018; David Maurice Smith/The New York Times.

Contents

CHAPTER 3

Environmental Crisis in the 21st Century

CHAPTER 4

A Future Without Plastic?

Introduction

SINCE THE 1940S, plastic has been an enormous part of our world, providing structure to the home and allowing advancements in science and technology. In the 21st century, the catastrophic effect of disposable plastics has become startlingly clear, wreaking havoc on our environment. The articles collected here recount the history of the plastics industry and suggest what the future may hold, including attempts to make plastic more biodegradable, the introduction of alternative materials and innovations in recycling.

In the early 20th century, advancements in chemical technology catalyzed innovations in the plastics industry, with mass production beginning in the middle of the century. Plastics manufacturing quickly became a significant component of the chemical industry, and some of the world's largest chemical companies, such as Dow Chemical, were involved since the earliest days. It was not long before plastic was everywhere.

Due to their affordability, versatility and relatively easy production, plastics are used in a variety of manufactured products of all different kinds, from household goods to computers and airplanes. Plastics provide architectural structure to buildings and have many uses in the field of medicine. The flexibility and malleability of plastic during manufacture means it can be configured in a variety of ways: It can be cast or extruded into many different shapes and forms, such as films, fibers, bottles and boxes. This incredibly versatile material quickly became the preference over traditional materials such as wood, stone, leather and glass.

Plastic frequently takes the form of disposable goods, such as shopping bags and food containers. Once these products have performed

An inmate picks up litter, including plastic bottles, at a dump site in Hickman County, Tenn., May 14, 2019.

their function, however, the rate of decomposition is remarkably slow. Plastics are synthetic polymers derived from petrochemicals, so it is very difficult for organic matter to penetrate and catalyze the process of breaking down plastic into smaller components. Since the earliest days of plastic production, environmentalists have questioned the sustainability of plastic, and voiced the potential risks of reliance on this synthetic material. Widespread excitement over this incredibly adaptable product initially quelled those who voiced concern over our growing dependence on plastic.

The rapid ascent of the plastic industry in the 20th century, and relatively sudden ubiquity of plastic products, led to widespread environmental concerns regarding their slow decomposition rate. As the 20th century came to a close, decades worth of "disposable" plastics began to clog landfills and fill the oceans. The 21st century has seen a full-on environmental crisis. Whales and sea turtles wash up on beaches, killed by the floating plastic debris they have swallowed. Even microplastics — pieces of plastic that are less than 0.2 inches long — pose threats to marine life and are difficult to collect from ocean waters. One study in 2017 found microplastics to be present in tap water samples from around the world. Another study in 2018 found evidence of microplastics in the digestive systems of people from eight different countries. Microplastics are also part of something known as the Great Pacific Garbage Patch — an area in the Pacific Ocean that has been collecting waste and becoming, as journalist Livia Albeck-Ripka writes, "a swirling oceanic graveyard where everyday objects get deposited by the currents."

This tragedy has been met by efforts to reduce plastic consumption, particularly of single-use plastics, and new solutions for reusing and recycling plastic material. The following stories examine the rise of plastics and the cultural and political forces driving the industry as well as provide tips for cutting down on plastic usage. They also highlight the environmental movement that arose in response and pose the question: Is a plastic-free future possible?

Fantastic Plastic

After World War II, advancements in chemical technology allowed for innovations in plastics manufacturing. Plastic became cheap and easy to produce, and it proved to be a useful and versatile material. Though excitement over this innovation initially dominated, the 1970s saw increased concern over the slow decomposition rate of plastic, and the alarming amount of pollution it created. As the environmental movement gained traction, however, it could not halt the rapid production of this now ubiquitous material.

Huge Role Played by Plastics in War

BY THE NEW YORK TIMES | **JAN. 3, 1943**

IN ITS ALL-OUT EFFORT to respond to the country's military needs last year, the plastics industry boosted the production of resins from about 450,000,000 pounds in 1941 to 600,000,000 pounds in 1942 and doubled in dollar value the output of molded and fabricated articles, according to a statement prepared exclusively for The New York Times by John M. Wetherby of the Society of the Plastics Industry. The dollar value of such products ran somewhere between $350,000,000 and $400,000,000.

"Certainly the past year has seen more diverse plastics applications and developments than ever before and the industry faces the future with a confidence born of meeting the rigid tests of war," Mr. Wetherby said.

Prior to the outbreak of war in Europe, he pointed out, the plastics industry had concerned itself mainly with the production of such everyday things as electrical appliances, radios, parts for automobiles, decorative buttons and hundreds of similar items designed for eye appeal and general civilian well-being.

ANSWERED CALL SPEEDILY

"Yet when the call came," Mr. Wetherby declared, "the industry responded with a speed and efficiency that has been one to marvel at. Its technicians knew in a general way the characteristics of the various plastics available and they immediately set out to adapt them to the requirements of all-out war. The armed services and other government branches cooperated closely, outlining their needs and computing available supplies, with results that are daily becoming more apparent.

"While all of the present uses of plastics cannot be detailed, for obvious reasons, some idea of the part which they are playing in our war effort may be gleaned from the fact that each of our new battleships incorporates well over 1,000 different plastic applications. The wide use of these materials in our aircraft is already pretty generally recognized, ranging all the way from the plastic bomber nose of high optical and aerodynamic qualities to the plastic bonded plywood fuselages and wings used on glider, trainer and freight-carrying planes. Today more than 200 different aircraft parts are being made from plastics and more are under development."

Not only have plastics proved to be desirable alternates for scarce metals where high tensile and impact strength is required; they are also being used to advantage in applications formerly associated with rubber, wood and glass, Mr. Wetherby said.

MATERIALS FOR CIVILIANS REDUCED

"The impact of our growing military demands upon the industry has naturally had far-reaching effects," Mr. Wetherby continued. "Many of the plastic materials formerly available for civilian application, are no longer to be had. One of the most critical of the plastic materials is to be found in the methacrylate resins, where all available current supplies are needed in war work. Methyl methacrylate is probably best known for its application in bomber noses, navigator domes and cockpit enclosures. New plants are being constructed and by the middle of 1943 output will be stepped up substantially. It is doubted, however, if the civilian can expect any more of this jewel-like product until after the war."

Plastics Gains Forecast

BY THE NEW YORK TIMES | MAY 26, 1943

Dr. Wendt sees new industries in the post-war period.

THE HUNDREDS OF varieties of plastics developed for war purposes, with their many thousands of uses, will ultimately lead to a great many new industries in the post-war era which will offer serious competition to the present types of textiles, Dr. Gerald D. Wendt, science editor of Time magazine, declared yesterday at the luncheon of the Sales Executives Club in the Hotel Roosevelt.

Referring to synthetic rubber as actually "one of those elastic but soft plastics," Dr. Wendt urged business men to turn their thoughts now into devising appropriate and acceptable names for the new wartime products of science. He recalled that under its original name, artificial silk did not attract as much interest on the part of consumers as does the synthetic yarn industry's present rayon output.

Most of the raincoats being used by the Army are not rubber-treated garments, he pointed out, but represent new developments in the use of plastics on cotton fabrics.

New Process Cuts Costs of Plastics

BY THE NEW YORK TIMES | DEC. 7, 1943

A NEW METHOD for molding synthetic resins, which will reduce substantially plastics production costs and widen the market for plastics
products, was outlined yesterday by the American Chemical Society
at the Nineteenth Exposition of Chemical Industries which opened in
Madison Square Garden.

The process, known as "heatronic molding," which has been developed by the Bakelite Corporation since Pearl Harbor, has six distinct
advantages over prior methods, it was explained. The process employs
electrostatic heating of plastics prior to molding, which generates heat
uniformly within the material by a high frequency electric field.

This uniform preheating, it was said, has brought down plastics
production costs and results in better manufacture since it reduces
molding time from minutes to seconds, permits much lower molding
pressures, eliminates limitations on thickness and size of moldings,
increases production of molds up to ten times of former capacity, produces moldings of greater uniformity and makes possible a universal
molding method.

The exposition, which features exhibits by approximately 200 companies, which will run through Saturday, is open only to executives
and personnel in plants with an interest in the chemical industry. However, much of the presentation relates to machinery and manufacturing equipment, with technical and research apparatus, instruments,
controls and processing materials emphasized.

Among the machinery displays Baker Perkins, Inc., presented a
newly developed "wet churn" which, it was said, will find extended use
in rayon-producing plants in the future. The machine, which carries a
xanthating reaction under vacuum and transfers cellulose xanthate
with its alkalin solvent directly to dissolving apparatus through closed
connections, is now coming into production. New type spinnerettes

used in the manufacture of yarn were displayed by Baker & Co., Inc. These spinnerettes, it was said, will cut "rejects" in rayon-yarn production and thus increase output.

Sutton, Steele & Steele, Inc., displayed an "air table" for separating foods, ores and other materials from wastes, which is finding increased use in plants for the recovery of scarce materials from wastes or by-products. Company officials stated they anticipate a broad market for such machines in Europe when better food production is sought. In addition this company and Ritter Products Corporation displayed electrostatic separation machines, screenless and vibrationless equipment capable of greater recovery of ores or producing maximum grade concentrates.

United States Stoneware displayed four new developments, including a new low-porosity chemical stoneware that is capable of withstanding violent heat shocks, a flexible boltless coupling for stoneware, or asbestos-cement pipe, and a bonding process that develops a bond stronger than the materials it joins.

An exhibit by the Army's Chemical Warfare Service featured the latest in smoke, flame and gas productive equipment and weapons. Other chemical devices shown include a new chemical mortar, portable flame throwers, impermeable clothing worn by decontamination crews, assorted incendiary bombs and hand grenades, smoke pots and portable chemical cylinders.

Rise in Chemicals Is Causing Alarm

BY RICHARD D. LYONS | SEPT. 26, 1971

WASHINGTON, SEPT. 25 — The vast array of man-made chemicals such as PCH, DDT, DDE and 2, 4, 5-T that are turning up increasingly in every nook and corner of the globe is producing outcries of alarm from scientists, ecologists and Congressmen.

This week, for example, Representative Peter H. B. Frelinghuysen, Republican of New Jersey, and 10 colleagues in the House proposed legislation that would require the registration and testing of all new chemicals before they are placed on the market. Their proposal was a reaction to the Federal Government's reversal of policy on the use of phosphate detergents.

It is essential that any chemical compounds destined for wide use be thoroughly tested as a matter of routine, rather than by accident," Mr. Frelinghuysen stated. He said about 250,000 new compounds were developed annually in this country alone.

Mr. Frelinghuysen noted that the detergent industry had spent about $1-billion seeking to replace phosphates with the now-suspect chemical NTA and said his bill would provide "an alternative to the current situation where either the public or industry can be big losers."

RAPID DEVELOPMENT

The last century has seen tremendously rapid development of organic chemistry with products such as pharmaceuticals that can cure and pollutants such as the benzopyrenes that can kill.

The insecticide DDT is estimated to have saved 500 million lives by containing the mosquitos that transmit malaria. But the price is DDT in everything, from food to the winds over the Sahara Desert to the tissues of penguins living in Antarctica.

While DDT is lethal in many forms of animal life, it is not believed to be harmful to man. Many of its sister chemicals are, however, and more are being held suspect, such as the phosphate replacement NTA, the herbicide 2,4,5-T and the plasticizer PCH.

These agents are known to produce cancers or birth defects in animal life. Scientists are seeking a link to human ills, and they are having a difficult time.

Arrayed against them are at least several million different substances, most of which have come into use only recently. In addition to the synthetic organic chemicals that are prime suspects as health hazards, the heavy metals, such as mercury, lead and cadmium and their compounds, are coming under increasing scrutiny.

Only when a gross example of environmental contamination occurs, such as the deaths of dozens of Japanese who ate fish tainted by methyl mercury, is the problem dramatized.

Some scientists believe that the as yet unseen and undetected hazards from the cumulative effects of small amounts of these compounds may be serious, especially in birth defects caused by the mother's exposure to the agents while she was pregnant.

Dr. Samuel E. Epstein, the professor of environmental health at Case Western Reserve Medical School in Cleveland who first called attention to the dangers of NTA, said, "It is impossible to answer the question of whether the chemical reservoir is harming the population because we have no hard data on things like birth defects."

"There is no question in my mind that the severe birth defects caused by thalidomide would have gone undetected for years but for one factor: the types of defects thalidomide caused [stunting of the arms and legs] were as rare as a dodo. They had hardly ever been seen before," he said.

TIP OF THE ICEBERG

"At the present moment there is no basis for expressing any opinion on whether birth defects are increasing or decreasing," he said. "There is the likelihood that there is a large reservoir of birth defects caused by these chemicals, many unrecognized. The tip of the iceberg shows only through specialized incidents.

"It might take 20, 30 or 40 years to document the causal relationships between birth defects and chemical exposure, especially since women are exposed to such a wide range of chemicals in the environment," he added. "What we need is a mandatory national registration of all birth defects through an examination of every newborn."

The largest examination of birth defects and their causes, involving 50,000 American mothers and their offspring, is being carried out by the National Institutes of Health. But the $100-million study, which has gone on for 13 years, was not designed to explore environmental contaminants.

Another method is being tried by the National Foundation-March of Dimes. It is aiding Dr. Vergil Slee of Ann Arbor, Mich., to computerize birth defect data on about one-third of the nation's births.

According to Dr. Virginia Apgar of the foundation: "We don't have a baseline for birth defects yet — but we're going to get it."

No Road Back to Natural Materials

OPINION | BY F. PERRY WILSON | MARCH 30, 1975

WITH THE ADVENT of the energy crisis, a new chorus of Cassandras has emerged who would have us believe that the nation is teetering on the edge of disaster.

Their visions of doom are based on the notion that there is a "fault" in our economy that places profits above energy efficiency. According to them, our salvation depends on a return to natural materials (leather, cotton, soap and wood) in place of man-made materials (chemical fertilizers, synthetic fibers, detergents and plastics).

This view is simplistic. Man-made materials are not in themselves more profitable nor does their manufacture and use necessarily involve more energy consumption than their natural equivalents.

The energy savings presumed to be involved in the substitution of paper for plastics or soap for detergents are a case in point. It takes more energy to make a paper bag than a polyethylene sack of the same capacity. It takes twice as much energy to make a nonreturnable glass bottle than most plastic containers of the same capacity. Detergents make possible cold water laundry washing and potential energy savings of 100,000 barrels of oil to the nation annually.

The same energy relationship is true of chemical fertilizers. Approximately 20 times as much manure is required to achieve the same nutrient plant value as a given unit of chemical fertilizer. Even if this option were open to us, the energy consumption required to collect, process and distribute it would be prohibitively expensive and the environmental problems involved would be staggering.

More importantly, chemical fertilizers are a key element in America's ability to feed 25 percent of the people of the world with only one-tenth of 1 percent of the planet's population employed on this nation's farms. The efficiency involved in such a proportion is unparalleled in history.

The impact on the nation's food production would be similarly hampered by the substitution of natural fibers for synthetics. Currently, about 70 percent of the nation's fiber production is man-made. If we were to revert to natural fibers — mainly cotton and some wool — the nation would require at least 13 million acres of additional farmland, much of which would have to be withdrawn from food production.

The effect would be higher prices and reduced supplies, dismal prospects for American consumers already beset by high food bills and for the hungry nations of the world who look to the United States for assistance.

The nostalgic notion of returning to simpler products and a simpler way of life is probably rooted in the popular belief that our resources can be consumed over greater spans of time while economic growth is reduced or stabilized.

But as Prof. Wilfred Beckerman of the University of London recently wrote, "The whole of the 'finite resources' argument against continued economic growth is based on a series of logical muddles, dubious moral judgments, a scant respect for the historical facts and a complete ignorance of the way that economies adjust to changes in demand and supply."

If there is a fault in the nation's current energy situation, it is the result of a patchwork of long-standing national policies that have held energy prices at unrealistic levels. These prices discouraged the exploration for new oil and gas reserves and hindered the development of the nation's ample coal supplies.

With the quadrupling of international oil prices there are indications that the laws of supply and demand are beginning to come into play. In fact, a significant excess of supply seems to be developing. Although it is too early to say with any degree of certainty, the recent discoveries in Mexico, China and off the coast of Norway and South Vietnam may in future years dilute the Organization of the Petroleum Exporting Countries' capacity to control world oil prices.

With some 90 percent of the exploratory drilling in the world now occurring outside these countries, the probability of finding new oil elsewhere is proportionately greater.

Nevertheless, it will take massive amounts of capital to achieve a reasonable balance between the nation's energy consumption and energy supplies. In its most fundamental sense, prices and profits are the basic issues in our long-term energy situation. But to attempt to remove profits from the mechanism that produces them is to throttle the very energizing factor in our economic system.

Far from favoring less efficient uses of energy, unregulated pricing would help curb uneconomic consumption while providing the means to marshal the needed development capital. Doomsaying will not raise that capital nor will the demolition of the American competitive enter-prise system — a system that is still the envy of the world.

F. PERRY WILSON is chairman of the Union Carbide Corporation.

The Promise and Perils of Petrochemicals

BY BARRY COMMONER | SEPT. 25, 1977

The petrochemical industry, that elegant new alchemy of our times, dramatizes the paradox of modern technology: its blessings are mixed with plagues.

THE ANCIENT GOAL of alchemy, turning baser metals into gold, can now be achieved by modern atom-smashing techniques, but the expense is prohibitive. However, where classical alchemy has failed to meet the test of the marketplace, that elegant new alchemy of our times — the petrochemical industry — has succeeded.

The petrochemical industry's products, made chiefly out of crude oil and natural gas, make up a marvelous catalogue of useful materials: cloth with the sheen of silk or the fuzziness of wool; cables stronger than steel; synthetics with the elasticity of rubber, the flexibility of leather, the lightness of paper, or the workableness of wood; detergents that wash as well as soap without curdling in hard water; chemicals that can kill dandelions, but not grass; repel mosquitoes, but not people; diminish sniffles, reduce blood pressure, or cure tuberculosis.

But something has gone wrong. Increasingly, the chemist succeeds, brilliantly, in synthesizing a new, useful, highly competitive substance, only to have it cast aside because of its biological hazards: Food dyes and fire-retardants for children's sleepwear are banned because they may cause cancer; a new industry to produce plastic soda bottles, developed at a cost of $50 million, comes to an abrupt halt as the Food and Drug Administration discovers that a chemical which may leach out of the bottles causes tumors in mice; pesticides are taken off the market because they kill fish and wildlife; firemen would like to ban plastic building materials because they produce toxic fumes when they burn.

The petrochemical industry, by any ordinary criteria — its rate of growth, its profitability, the apparent eagerness of consumers to purchase huge quantities of its products — is the most successful in postwar America. Yet it is now caught by forces that threaten its viability. The industry's raw materials, petroleum and natural gas — once cheap and plentiful — are now becoming astronomically expensive as the supplies shrink and become increasingly uncertain. The industry has been beset by Federal regulations and by pressure from the public, often based on the widespread fear of cancer, to control not only the dissemination of its toxic wastes, but also of some of the industry's most salable products, such as saccharin. These pressures on a major American industry have important implications for the economy, for the availability of jobs, for the future of industrial technology, and will affect the availability of products that most of us have taken for granted, and may soon have to do without.

THE PETROCHEMICAL INDUSTRY is a huge success in the marketplace. Since World War II, the industry's detergents have driven soap out of a market that it monopolized for perhaps a thousand years; in textiles, synthetic fibers have massively displaced cotton and wool; plastics have replaced long-established uses of metals, wood and glass; food production has become heavily dependent on fertilizers, pesticides and other agricultural chemicals; synthetic drugs and toiletries have become a major enterprise in an area of commerce once represented by concoctions of herbs.

In most industrial nations the petrochemical industry has become the fastest-growing sector of manufacturing. In the United States, in the last 30 years, it has grown at an annual rate of about 8 percent, twice the rate of growth of manufacturing industries as a whole. The industry's economic rewards have been correspondingly large: In that period its rate of profit has generally led those of all major industries; and the pharmaceuticals have led all the rest, recording profits ranging about 20 percent, as compared with the 11 percent average for manufacturing as a whole.

Yet the petrochemical industry dramatizes the paradox of modern technology: Its blessings are mixed with plagues. Here are some of the more recent troubles:

• In Michigan, because a chemical plant inadvertently combined a fire-retardant with animal feed, thousands of cattle and millions of chickens were lost, and hundreds of people made ill.

• In Virginia, because of the careless operation of a small insecticide plant, the entire Chesapeake Bay fishing industry has been threatened, and dozens of chemical workers have had their health ruined.

• In Seveso, Italy — a small town near Milan — the accidental release of a few pounds of a highly toxic chemical from a petrochemical plant has caused serious illness among hundreds of children and forced the evacuation, now in its second year, of 700 people from their homes.

The most chilling prospect is that much of the cancer problem in the United States may eventually be laid at the door of the petrochemical industry. The most drastic actions taken against the petrochemical industry thus far — the banning of DDT and other chlorinated hydrocarbon insecticides, and most recently PCB — have been largely based on their hazards as possible carcinogens. It has been estimated that perhaps three-fourths of the incidence of cancer in the United States is due to environmental agents, and a recent county-by-county survey of cancer incidence shows a significant correlation with the local concentrations of petrochemical operations. The highest incidence of bladder cancer in the United States is found in Salem County, N.J., an area dense with refineries and petrochemical plants. A particularly alarming fact is that since the 1960's the downward trend in the death rate among United States males has stopped and reversed itself, and according to a recent U.S. Public Health Service survey, cancers (other than those attributed to smoking) are prominent among the causes of the rising death rate. Since many cancers may develop only

An aerial view of the sprawling Monsanto Petrochemical Complex in Texas City, Tex.

10 years or more after exposure to the instigating substance, and since widespread exposure to petrochemical products has occurred only in the last 20 to 25 years, there is reason to fear that these changes may foreshadow an upsurge in the incidence of cancer. If so, we may be facing an epidemic of environmental cancer, induced by past, irremediable exposures to petrochemicals.

The quandary of the petrochemical industry is that the unique reasons for its success and growth — that it can produce a growing variety of new man-made substances, and can sell them cheaply, but only in very large amounts — are themselves the sources of its growing threat to society. Pressed by its economic structure to create ever more chemically complex man-made products on huge scales, the industry now confronts a hard fact of nature — that the more complex these products, the more likely they are to harm living things, including people, and the more widespread they are, the greater their toxic impact.

THE PETROCHEMICAL INDUSTRY is fundamentally different from all other production industries. To begin with, it is a *process* industry. This sets it off from ordinary manufacturing such as the production of automobiles, dresses or frying pans. In these enterprises, the *form* of the final product is different from that of the starting materials, but the substances of which it is made — steel, glass and rubber; cotton, wool or nylon; iron or aluminum — remain unchanged. In contrast, in a process industry a new substance is produced: Iron ore, coke and oxygen, properly combined, become steel; sand and lime, heated together, become glass; two petrochemicals, butadiene and styrene, appropriately reacted, become synthetic rubber.

However, where the other process industries produce only a few different types of steel or glass, the petrochemical industry converts oil and natural gas into many hundreds of chemically different substances. The industry is based on the chemistry of the carbon atom, which can combine in enormously variable ways with the other atoms that most frequently occur in carbon-containing compounds, hydrogen, oxygen and nitrogen. The industry's processes branch like some great genealogical tree: From crude oil, which contains 10 major primary constituents, the industry produces about 75 chief intermediate chemicals, which are converted into about 100 large-scale end products, each manufactured in amounts ranging from one million to three billion pounds per year. At each successive stage, the industry produces more numerous, more varied, and, as we shall see, more dangerous substances.

Materials flow constantly through the industry's gargantuan network of multiply interconnected pipelines, separators and reactors. Since storage is very expensive and therefore limited in capacity, everything that enters the system has to go somewhere: It is either carted off as a final product, burned by the industry itself as a fuel (or wastefully as a "flare") or — too often — expelled into the environment as waste.

The petrochemical industry has a strong, built-in tendency to proliferate, to elaborate the number and variety of its products. Consider what happened when the industry began to market one of its most successful products, polyethylene film — that ubiquitous wrapping around everything from supermarket beefsteaks to kitchen leftovers. Through the strange, Rube Goldberg economics of the petrochemical industry, acrylic fiber captured the rug market largely because supermarkets began to use huge amounts of polyethylene film to wrap vegetables and cuts of meat. It happened this way: The film is manufactured from ethylene. Ethylene production yields, as a major byproduct, propylene. At first, this was burned by the industry as a fuel. But then it was discovered that propylene could be converted to acrylonitrile, which could then be used to manufacture acrylic fibers for rugs. When propylene was sold for that purpose, it brought a price twice its value as fuel. This saving significantly reduced the cost of producing ethylene, ultimately cutting the price of polyethylene film as well, and expanding its sales. Therefore, at the same time, acrylic fiber was marketable at an attractive price because it could be produced cheaply and in large amounts.

Thus, new products are often created not so much to meet the consumer's needs as the industry's. This approach is clearly reflected in a typical petrochemical company's (the Hooker Chemical Company) research policy: "Rather than manufacturing known products by a known method for a known market ... the research department is now free to develop any product that looks promising. If there is not a market for it, the sales development group seeks to create one."

This helps to explain why petrochemical products characteristically *invade* the rest of the production system. Since synthetic detergents appeared in the 1940's, they have captured about 85 percent of the market once held by soap. Since 1950, synthetic fibers have taken over about 70 percent of the United States textile market, once largely held by cotton and wool. The production of plastics has grown at the rate of 16 percent per year, while the production of competitive materials has been much slower: Leather has increased at an annual rate of only 1.2 percent, paper at 4.8 percent, and lumber production has decreased at a rate of 0.5 percent per year.

The petrochemical industry seems to have developed a kind of economic imperialism, forcing consumers to give up old products, most of them natural, for synthetic replacements. If this judgment seems harsh, it is nevertheless shared by one of the leaders of the British petrochemical industry, Lord Beeching: "Instead of producing known products to satisfy existing industrial needs, it [the petrochemical industry] is, increasingly, producing new forms of matter which not only replace the materials used by existing industries, but which cause extension and modification of those industries. … To an increasing degree it forces existing industries to adapt themselves to use its products." The truth of Lord Beeching's generalization is evident to anyone who has recently tried to find a pure cotton shirt, a laundry cleaner free of synthetics, or a wooden clothespin.

The rapidly changing energy situation is likely to intensify these problems. Fearing a shortage of natural gas, a large sector of the petrochemical industry is planning to substitute crude oil as a source of ethylene. This switch will demand new capital investments that are three to four times greater than current investments in natural gas-based facilities, no small feat in a period of capital shortage. Using crude oil for ethylene production will mean that many more leftover chemicals will be produced, and, according to a recent analysis of the situation in Business Week, "a much wider variety of products." Not surprisingly, Edward G. Jefferson, senior vice president of DuPont, sees this new situation as "one in which the petrochemical industry becomes an even more important mainstay of the United States economy." Once more, the peculiar technological and economic design of the petrochemical industry forces it to proliferate new products and to penetrate more deeply into the national economy.

The petrochemical invasion has been particularly targeted against the largest, most long-established markets — for clothing, building materials, furniture, appliances, cleansers and other necessities. These invasions succeed because synthetic petrochemical products can be manufactured in large volumes at low prices. This capability is, in turn, the outcome of the technological design of the petrochemical industry. The machinery used in the flow processes that characterize petrochemical production is very complex, replete with miles of piping, specially built reactor vessels, numerous valves, switches, recording devices and elaborate controls. The machinery is very expensive; the petrochemical industry is the most capital intensive of all major manufacturing industries, producing only about 80 cents of value added per dollar of capital invested, as compared with about $3.64, in the case of a typical natural competitor, the leather industry. Since the size and the output of a petrochemical plant can be increased a great deal without a proportional increase in the numbers of expensive valves and controls — or in the amount of labor needed to operate them — there is a considerable economy of scale. A large investment in machinery is more profitable than a small one. As a result, large petrochemical plants are much more economically efficient than small ones. If the capacity of a typical petrochemical plant is increased from one million to 10 million pounds per year, the cost of manufacturing a pound of product is reduced by two thirds. Thus, petrochemical products can he sold at a low price, but only in very large amounts.

This gives the petrochemical industry a powerful economic advantage in invading large, well-developed markets such as the clothing field. These markets usually exhibit what economists call a "high elasticity of demand": Demand for a particular product rises disproportionately with a fall in price, and vice versa. Synthetic fibers and plastics can readily invade such a market by selling at the low prices made possible by the economies of scale and the by-product development typical of the petrochemical industry. Thus, between 1960 and 1970, as the price of polyvinyl chloride fell by 75 percent, consumption increased by 500 percent, enabling the plastic to replace leather in clothes, handbags, shoes and gloves.

For all these reasons, the economic success of the petrochemical industry has been a self-fulfilling prophecy. Once the industry became established, it was bound to grow, and, by further reducing prices, growth carried the industry into new markets, further accelerating its expansion. The industry would appear to be an invincible competitor in the marketplace of a free economy.

Yet the industry has been increasingly vulnerable to the dangers inherent in its own product ion processes. That the industry itself has thus far been unable to reduce its hazards to a level acceptable to the public is evident from the intensely critical response to recent environmental catastrophes. The Kepone accident, for example, resulted in an unprecedented fine — $13 million — levied against the Allied Chemical Corporation for its responsibility in the disaster; civil suits involved more than $100 million in damage claims.

Additional evidence that the industry itself can no longer cope with the growing risks inherent in its operations is found in its insurance record. Ordinarily, commercial enterprises protect themselves against such risks by obtaining insurance to cover the expected cost of possible damages. When the risk and the possible damage are high, the premium is large; when the possible damage is very great, and difficult to compute accurately, insurance is usually unobtainable. In recent years, the petrochemical industry has suffered from both of these difficulties. A recent survey of the problem in Chemical & Engineering News complains of "skyrocketing insurance premiums, with renewals sometimes 30 to 50 times higher than the old rate. Policies canceled, often without notice or reason. Throughout the industry, companies are finding it increasingly difficult to obtain product liability insurance."

Two of the petrochemical industry's trade associations have considered establishing their own insurance companies, somewhere in the Bahamas. Another proposed solution is no-fault insurance possibly based on a Federal insurance company. Like the nuclear-power industry before it (which, by virtue of the Price Anderson Act, is now provided with Federal insurance coverage against the huge damage that might result from an accident), the petrochemical industry may find it necessary to shift the burden of insurance risks from its own, private responsibility, to society's.

Meanwhile, some of the industry's earlier economic advantages have backfired. Originally, the industry's raw materials, petroleum and natural gas, were plentiful and available at a constant price. Now the situation is dramatically different. With the energy crisis, the industry's dependence on these fuels has become a serious economic liability, as supplies become shaky and their costs rise at an astronomical rate. At the same time, the petrochemical industry may be particularly vulnerable to the growing shortage of investment capital. The industry's vaunted high labor productivity, which is nearly three times the average for that of all manufacturing industries, is achieved at the expense of very intense investments of capital.

THE CLASH BETWEEN the economic success of synthetic petrochemicals and their increasing vulnerability to biological complaints is the inevitable result of the very fact that the petrochemicals are synthetic — made by man, not nature. In every living cell there is a tightly integrated network of chemical processes which has evolved over three billion years of trial and error. In all of the countless organisms that have lived over this time, and in all of their even more numerous separate cells, there has been a huge number of opportunities for chemical errors — the production of substances that could disrupt the delicately balanced chemistry of the living cell. Like other evolutionary misfits, any organism that made these chemical mistakes perished, so that the genetic tendency to produce the offending substance was eliminated from the line of evolutionary descent. One can imagine that at some point in the course of evolution some unfortunate cell managed to synthesize, let us say, DDT — and became a casualty in the evolutionary struggle to survive.

Another requirement for evolutionary survival is that every substance synthesized by living things must be broken down by them as well — be biodegradable. It is this biological rule which establishes the distinctive closed cycles of ecology. When petrochemical technology synthesizes a new complex substance that is alien to living things, they are likely to lack the enzymes needed to degrade the substance — which then accumulates as waste. This explains why our beaches have become blanketed in debris, since nondegradable synthetics have replaced hemp cordage, wooden spoons and paper cups, which, because they were made of natural cellulose, soon decayed.

The likelihood that a synthetic organic chemical will be biologically hazardous increases with its complexity; the more elaborate its structure, the more likely that some part of it will be incompatible with the normal chemistry of life. While only 10 percent of the relatively simple primary constituents of petroleum and natural gas are classified as "highly toxic," by the time the petrochemical tree has branched several times to yield much more complex products, the proportion of highly toxic substances has increased to about 50 percent. Thus, as the petrochemical industry is forced by the logic of its economic design to produce increasing numbers of ever more complex synthetic substances, it also increases the risk that some of these products will be dangerous to living things

As the uses of a product expand, it comes in contact with people in rapidly increasing numbers and in new ways. Then, the built-in propensity of man-made organic chemicals to cause biological troubles has many new opportunities to express itself. Unfortunately, the industry does not readily respond to this change. According to a recent Environmental Protection Agency survey, as production expands "… there is essentially no mechanism that triggers expanded toxicological and environmental testing. Such expanded testing, when it occurs, is nearly always in response to a reaction to some adverse finding outside the company." The survey points out, for example, that although United States production of vinyl chloride — a substance recently shown to cause cancer — increased from 321 million pounds in 1952 to 5,300 million pounds in 1973, the industry's assessment of the health hazard failed to keep up with the sharply increased human exposure "until after some adverse publications in the scientific literature," as the E.P.A. report says.

Nevertheless, whether heeded or not, the earliest warning that a petrochemical has a potential for large-scale disaster usually comes from *within* the industry: Chemical workers, who inevitably are most exposed to the substance, become ill. For example, production of PCB expanded from 20,000 tons in 1960 to 43,000 tons in 1970, although as early as 1941 the severe effects of PCB on workers' health had caused public-health officials to publish warnings that "human contact with PCB should be avoided." Had this admonition been heeded, the expanded use of PCB, especially in products accessible to human contact, such as plastics, paint, ink and paper, and its spread into the environment — not to speak of repeated industrial exposures — could have been avoided.

Such failures to appreciate in good time the biological hazards of petrochemicals are sometimes not so much a matter of neglect as of impotence. In some cases, analytical methods are unable to detect the very low levels at which many substances are toxic. For example, PCB was detectable in the environment only after chemical analysts learned how to separate it from its close relative, DDT. In other cases, as synthetic substances penetrate into the intricate network of the environment, they begin to interact, not only with natural substances but with each other, creating a statistical nightmare. Thus, many of the several hundred synthetic organic chemicals that now find their way into water supplies readily react with the chlorine used in water purification and form new substances, which may in turn react with each other. A common product of these reactions is chloroform, which has now become the most ubiquitous synthetic organic pollutant of United States water supplies; it is a carcinogen. In the area of Charleston, W. Va., where seven large petrochemical plants and several smaller ones annually emit tons of waste substances into the air, 128 different synthetic organic compounds have been identified among them. Several of the waste substances can cause cancer and birth defects. No one knows how many other hazardous substances are produced by the further reaction that may occur among the original pollutants, once they mix in the air.

THE MOST SERIOUS threat to the petrochemical industry is that society is becoming less willing to bear the "externalities" — the risks that the industry has imposed on society as a result of its private success. The strongest evidence is the recent passage of the Toxic Substances Control Act late in 1976. The act empowers the administrator of the Environmental Protection Agency to regulate the manufacture and distribution of chemical substances judged to "present an unreasonable risk of injury to health or the environment." In reaching this judgment, the administrator must conduct open hearings, in which all interested parties, including public-interest and citizens' groups, can participate, with Federal financial assistance, if needed. In establishing a rule to govern a particular substance, the administrator must consider not only its hazard to health and the environment, but also its benefits, the availability of substitutes which are less hazardous, the "reasonably ascertainable economic consequences of the rule ..." and its "social impact."

Given this broad mandate for an open discussion of a substance's biological hazards and its economic and social virtues and faults as compared with those of alternatives, this new legislation may result in two very different outcomes for the petrochemical industry and for society.

One possible outcome is that enforcement of the act will become bogged down in niggling debates over what constitutes "an unreasonable risk of injury" and over the comparable benefits of each particular substance. Predictably, industry representatives will argue that the risk of injury is insignificant, while public-interest groups will argue the opposite. Test results will be debated; analytical methods questioned; statistics compared. In view of the enormous number of substances to be considered, running into the thousands, it is easy to envisage the end result of this approach. Substance by substance, disputed judgments of their hazards will slowly emerge from a vast bureaucratic jungle. It is to be hoped that this will gradually reduce the number of hazardous substances to which we are exposed. But it will do little to correct the problem at its source, which is that petro-chemical production is governed not so much by society's needs for the products as by the industry's need to make a profit by manufacturing a growing variety of substances in the largest possible amounts.

On the other hand, if sufficient attention is given to the act's broad mandate to compare the benefits and risks of a petrochemical product with those of available substitutes — including natural ones — and to consider the economic and social consequences of choosing between them, the hearings may have an entirely different outcome. Industry representatives are then likely to reiterate their belief in the benefits of their products, relative to the risks: that agricultural chemicals produce plentiful food at reasonable prices; that synthetic textiles produce affordable clothes which are easy to maintain; that plastic auto parts are lighter, stronger and cheaper than metal ones; that the construction of a plant to manufacture a new plastic substitute for leather will create new jobs. In rebuttal, their opponents may well reply that recent studies show that some commercial farmers do about as well with organic methods as their conventional neighbors who use chemicals, that cotton fabrics are much less energy intensive than synthetic ones (which are, after all, made from petroleum and natural gas); that the economic gains afforded by cheaper auto parts are offset by the economic drain imposed on a capital-short economy by the capital-intensive petrochemical industry; that because leather production is much more labor intensive than the petrochemical industry, the displacement of leather by a new plastic will reduce, rather than increase, the total number of available jobs.

Guided by this broader mandate, the Toxic Substances Control Act can do much more than regulate the use of hazardous materials. It can, in fact, open what the industry may regard as a political Pandora's box, providing an arena in which the public will be able to intervene effectively in a process that is normally the exclusive domain of industrial managers: decisions about what to produce and how to produce it.

This issue has already been raised in connection with nuclear power. Concern over its hazards has led to a growing demand for phasing out the industry: its social burden has generated a demand for social governance of the industry. Many Americans already hold strong opinions about one major petrochemical product, plastics. A recent public-opinion poll conducted for the Society of the Plastics Industry showed that, in comparison with alternative goods, many public officials regard plastics as the most hazardous alternative, and the product which they would be most willing to do without.

Based upon widespread concern over health and environmental problems, the public appears to be ready — as it is in the case of nuclear power — to determine what balance between the hazards and benefits of the petrochemical industry is acceptable. Not only in terms of health and the environment, but also in terms of the economy and social welfare; and not only of the petrochemical products themselves, but also in comparison with the alternative natural products which have been the chief victims of the industry's compulsive invasion of the economy.

In this way the Toxic Substances Control Act can facilitate a discussion which will enable the people of the United States to decide how to respond to the sweeping challenge of the petrochemical industry. Shall we establish another bureaucracy that attempts, in long and costly deliberations, to alleviate the hazards to health and the environment that are so closely associated with the petrochemical industry? Or shall we establish some means of social governance over the forces that compel the industry to bestow upon us, along with its benefits, the biological dangers that are inherent to an enterprise bent on confronting living things with substances that they, in their evolutionary wisdom, have long since rejected?

BARRY COMMONER is director of the Center for the Biology of Natural Systems at Washington University, St. Louis, Mo. He is chairman of the board of directors of the Scientists' Institute for Public Information and, most recently, the author of "The Poverty of Power."

A Closer Look At Ocean Pollution

BY JOANNE A. FISHMAN | APRIL 22, 1979

IN THE THREE YEARS since the massive summer fish kills along the New Jersey coast and the discovery of a 3,000-square-mile "dead sea" offshore, water conditions in the New York Bight have not improved. In fact, they are the same as they were a decade ago, according to marine scientists and environmentalists.

The bight, a 15,000-square-mile area between Long Island and New Jersey, remains the most severely polluted of the nation's coastal waters, the scientists say. Toxic chemicals pose a genuine, long-term threat, the experts add, and they contend that the only cure for these troubled waters is billions of dollars to develop and implement new technology for treating toxic wastes.

But the techniques for studying the water have changed dramatically. Marine scientists now are taking to the air for a better look at what is going on in the ocean.

The first large-scale experiment in air-sea monitoring of the ocean began last Tuesday and involved two aircraft from the National Aeronautics and Space Administration and 24 oceanographic research vessels. The planes, a U-2 and a C-130, flew from Cape Hatteras, N.C., to Maine in the course of the two-day project, photographing and scanning with sensors a 14-mile-wide swath of ocean. Aboard the ships, nearly 100 marine scientists took water and sediment samples.

The new approach is part of the comprehensive program of monitoring cruises called Ocean Pulse — a program that began in the bight in the wake of the disastrous water conditions in 1978. These were attributed to a combination of a vast algae "bloom," which reduced oxygen levels, and unusual currents, which pushed the mass of algae inshore from the continental shelf. Inshore, the algae fed on the high amounts of nutrients in the water caused by inadequately treated sewage, urban runoff and the dumping of sludge.

The air-sea program, termed the Large Area Marine Experiment, is a "grand-scale feasibility test," according to Dr. James Thomas, coordinator of the experiment and chief of biological oceanographic investigations for the Northeast Fisheries Center laboratories at Sandy Hook, N.J.

The ships and scientists have been drawn from nearly every major marine research center at universities in the Northeast as well as from Federal agencies and some state and local groups.

"It's the first real effort," Dr. Thomas said, "to bring the state universities and the Federal Government together in such a venture."

When the C-130 took off from NASA's Langley Research Center in Virginia last week, Dr. Thomas was aboard to calibrate data collected by the ships and the planes' electronic scanning devices. This procedure is designed to measure the amount of chlorophyll in the waters.

Photographs also will give the scientists a map of the bight showing the patterns of effluent that flow into the ocean from coastal rivers and bays. It will also show ocean "frontal systems" — masses of water that are pushed together by currents in much the same way that atmospheric frontal systems are driven by the wind. Where the systems meet, Dr. Thomas said, is often a collecting area for pollutants, suspended solids and chlorophyll, sometimes in the form of algae.

By tracking the chlorophyll in marine plants, which serve as food for many species of infant fish, scientists hope to develop better techniques for fishery management. Also, knowing the relation between the frontal system and the movement of coastal effluents will help explain the impact of pollutants, Dr. Thomas said.

This is especially significant in the bight, since 86 percent of all dumping of municipal and industrial waste in the United States occurs there.

While such sophisticated monitoring is geared to track down the visible pollution, scientists also agree that the pollution that cannot be detected may pose the greatest danger.

"Things are not getting better in the bight," said Capt. Lawrence

Swanson, who recently left his post as head of the National Oceanographic and Atmospheric Administration's New York Bight project at Stony Brook to head that agency's new Office of Marine Pollution Assessment. "Nothing's been removed one way or another. The toxic chemicals going into the system remain, and the same inefficiencies that existed a decade ago in the sewage system still exist."

"In the final analysis," he added, a cleanup "will be a costly affair and I'm not sure people are willing to pay the price."

"It's a matter of perception," Captain Swanson went on. "When it comes to their pocketbooks, people react negatively and the general quality of life continues to decrease."

Captain Swanson said he thought that Americans tend to "coast along until the situation is nearly hopeless, then go and do it." He added, "But, basically, the people will have to decide this, because to clean the apex of the bight will cost billions."

The apex is the triangle of water that reaches from New York City to Rockaway Point on Long Island and Sandy Hook in New Jersey, and includes the sludge-dump site 12 miles offshore.

"When we decide to improve the situation, we will have to pay the price for pre-treatment," Captain Swanson said. "We have to have more efficient sewage systems. We have to get the exotic materials, the synthetic organisms such as PCB's [polychlorinated biphenals] and heavy metals out of the waterways."

Traces of PCB's have been known to cause deformities in fetuses, changes in liver function, nervous disorders and cancers.

Studies done at the Sandy Hook laboratories have shown that the waters off Sandy Hook contain more copper than anywhere else in the world and that the presence of the metal is having an adverse affect on the growth of fish eggs and larvae.

Sediment in Raritan Bay has been found to contain heavy metals in such high concentrations that they are contaminating the marine food chain and, in some cases, wiping out certain forms of marine life there altogether.

Indeed, the level of heavy metals in the bight is higher than any-where else in the country, according to W. D. Bennett, executive direc-tor of the American Littoral Society, an international group concerned with coastal waters and based at Sandy Hook. But Mr. Bennett pointed out that no fish have yet been caught that contain high enough levels of toxins to have their consumption as food banned.

However, fish have been caught that show fin rot. Winter floun-der seem particularly prone to this ailment, Mr. Bennett said, adding that while tests had not conclusively shown a cause and effect process involving pollution, "the relationship is there. The higher incidence of diseased fish by far is found in polluted waters."

However, he added, no threat to human health is involved, since fish ailments cannot be transmitted to people.

In addition, irreversible damage has been observed in the surf clam population in the bight's apex. The clams, according to Captain Swanson, no longer grow to maturity.

Four factors are involved in assessing water conditions, Mr. Ben-nett said: the presence of "floatables," the visible garbage such as Styrofoam, plastic and oil globules; dissolved-oxygen levels, which naturally decline toward the end of summer as the water warms up; the presence of toxic chemicals and heavy metals, and the presence of nutrients, a consequence of inadequately treated sewage, urban runoff and the dumping of sludge.

Such nutrients are the source of viruses and bacteria. "They are in the water," Mr. Bennett said. "That's why clam beds in polluted waters are closed."

"The hepatitis virus in the water is from humans," he went on. "And there is no question that there are more human viruses and bacteria in the water here than there are in areas where you do not have 15 million people flushing their toilets into the water."

All municipalities and industries that use coastal waters for dump-ing are required to have a permit from the Federal Environmental Pro-tection Agency. A 1977 amendment to the Marine Protection, Research and Sanctuaries Act requires that the agency order the phase-out by 1981 of any ocean waste disposal operation that unreasonably degrades the marine environment.

But, in an apparent paradox, the E.P.A. last year permitted one concern, NL Industries of Sayville, to resume its dumping of acid waste in the bight. There is apparently no place on land for the company to safely dispose of its 4.5 million tons a year of sulfate acid and inert waste material.

But scientists and environmentalists agree that acid dumping is the least of their concerns, since acid is neutralized by the salts in seawater.

The only industries that apparently will be permitted to continue dumping in the bight after 1981, according to the E.P.A.'s timetable, are three chemical companies, including NL Industries. The other two are the Allied Chemical Company, which dumps hydrochloric acid, and DuPont-Grasselli, which dumps caustic soda.

Yet the real culprits, as far as the E.P.A. is concerned, are the municipalities because the toxins and viruses enter the water through sewage waste.

"Most municipalities believe the 1981 deadline is going to go away," said Dr. Richard Dewling, deputy administrator of the E.P.A.'s Region II, which encompasses the bight.

But the E.P.A., he said, is going to court to force compliance. Last November, the Justice Department filed charges against New York City and Westchester County for failing to meet schedules for ending ocean disposal. Currently, New York dumps 350 million gallons of raw sewage into the apex each day.

"The technical solution for municipalities is here," Dr. Dewling said, "and that means land, not ocean, disposal. What is not here is the institutional and social acceptance of that solution."

As Frank Steimle, a fishery biologist at the Sandy Hook labs, put it: "If the E.P.A. manages to remain firm about the 1981 deadline, then there's hope for the environment. It will take many years for the apex to bounce back, but nature is self-purifying. It will try to recover."

The chemical pollutants will still be in the sediments, but they would gradually be covered by silt. Bacteria and viruses, Mr. Steimle said, are not natural to the marine environment, and eventually should die out.

Mr. Bennett said that all the troubles in the bight affect people, whether they are viewed from the perspective of people deciding simply to stop going to the seashore because of pollution or "the other extreme, where there is nerve damage."

But such problems tend to be translated into costs. "If something costs $10 million to recycle," Mr. Bennett went on, "people ask, 'Does it do $10 million worth of damage offshore?' It's hard to say how much a person is worth."

Synthetics Go to New Lengths in Outperforming Natural Materials

BY MALCOLM W. BROWNE | MARCH 31, 1981

OFTEN BORROWING FROM the growing understanding of the chemistry of life, polymer scientists are creating new materials with such startling properties they promise technological changes comparable to ancient man's transition from stone to metal tools.

The new polymers — molecules consisting of very long chains of simple molecular groups — are close chemical relatives of the polymers used in plastic pens, bottles, furniture, synthetic textiles and the millions of other polymer-based products that have become familiar throughout the world since the 1940's. (The word "plastic" usually refers to a mixture of one or more polymers with other materials that make the mixture soft enough to mold into useful products.)

But while the older polymer-based plastics were mainly cheap replacements for natural substances, new polymers can do things far beyond the reach of conventional materials.

Some of the new polymers are so strong that they outperform steel as motorcycle sprockets, engine parts, deep-sea drilling cables and self-lubricating bearings. Engineers even envision a polymer cable so much lighter and stronger than steel it might be used to connect a geosynchronous space satellite with a ground station, permitting future astronauts to ride into space on elevators.

Various new polymers contain electrons that are free to wander, and they therefore conduct electricity like metals. Some may form the basis of a new generation of high-performance storage batteries with nonmetal electrodes. Others, capable of transforming various kinds of energy into electricity, may be developed for cheap photovoltaic cells harnessing sunlight. Even a polymer-based photovoltaic paint may be made some day, able to transform an entire house into a solar generator of electricity.

Special polymer films are being used to separate salt from sea-water in irrigation projects and promise to reduce the cost of manufacturing many basic chemicals.

Future engineering of polymer molecules that mimic living substances may one day lead to bizarre applications. One, artificial muscle, was mentioned in an interview by Howard E. Simmons, director of central research and development at E.I. Du Pont de Nemours & Company in Wilmington, Del.

"Animal muscle tissue is made largely of natural polymers," he said, "and one of the dreams of the polymer chemist is to make synthetic muscle. I could even imagine a car propelled by synthetic muscles made of polymers. A continuously changing bath of electrolyte solutions might cause the polymers to contract and relax, providing the motive force." Such polymers might be in the form of coiled springs, similar to certain natural proteins in which slight chemical changes can cause coiling and uncoiling.

Scientists at the Massachusetts Institute of Technology and Massachusetts General Hospital recently reported success in developing an artificial human skin. Made from synthetic polymers, it has many of the characteristics of natural skin and protects burn victims from infection during healing.

Most synthetic polymers used to replace blood vessels and other parts of a living circulatory system cause blood to clot. But at Research Triangle Institute in North Carolina, an electric-discharge method has been developed for depositing a thin coating of specially engineered molecules, which apparently eliminates the clotting problem. Scientists believe this may lead to much wider use of synthetic polymers to replace body parts.

Distinctions between "life" chemistry and the chemistry of synthetic polymers have become blurred by scientific advances. It is now understood that the protein building blocks of life, including the molecules of DNA, or deoxyribonucleic acid, that transmit the genetic code from parents to offspring, are complex polymers.

Scientists have been researching possibilities for artificial hearts for decades. Dr. Robert K. Jarvik, who designed the University of Utah mechanical heart of plastic, is seen here with the calf that lived for 268 days with the machine beating in the place of its heart. Dr. Jarvik holds the plastic heart device in hand.

"We're likely to create polymers with very interesting characteristics once we discover how to use the double helical coil structure of DNA in synthetics," one chemist said.

A survey made last year by the American Chemical Society found polymer chemists among the scientists most sought by American employers. But polymer chemistry got off to a slow start.

As laboratory curiosities, synthetic polymers have been known since 1839, when styrene was first polymerized in a laboratory. But it was only in 1907, when Leo Baekeland reacted carbolic acid with formaldehyde to make Bakelite, that the first commercial plastic came into being.

The making of a polymer material entails assembling links of simple molecular fragments into chains, then arranging the chains in interconnected networks.

CARBON IS VERSATILE

By far the most versatile building block for these chains is the element carbon, whose ability to join with itself and other atoms in many different ways is unique. The electronic structure of carbon atoms makes them the equivalent of end connectors in a Tinkertoy.

Of more than five million chemical compounds known to science, all but a small minority contain carbon. The potential of carbon to form an immense diversity of compounds is regarded by biologists as the fundamental reason that life was able to begin and evolve on our planet.

Typical of industrial polymerization is the building of chains from the colorless gas ethylene, which consists of two carbon atoms linked to two hydrogen atoms. Using heat, pressure and catalysts (materials that promote chemical reactions), repeating links of ethylene can be forged together into chains 40,000 or more units long.

These spaghetti-like chains may come into such close contact with each other that electronic forces between some of their atoms lock them into a three-dimensional form, like the steel reinforcing rods in structural concrete. The resulting substance, called polyethylene, is tough and waxy-feeling, and is used to make trash bags, orange juice bottles and countless other things.

MODIFICATIONS WITH FLUORINE

Branches can be attached to various links along the backbone of a polymer chain, changing its physical characteristics. Changes can also be made by inserting different atoms or molecular links at key points. The substitution of fluorine for some of the atoms in a polymer chain, for instance, often produces great resistance to chemicals, heat or wetting, as in the Teflon used to line nonstick frying pans. Subtle techniques for making such molecular modifications are the key competitive assets of plastics manufacturers.

Sometimes researchers discover polymers that offer immense improvements over existing materials but are so difficult to make into anything useful that they find no immediate application. Such was the case in the 1950's with a class of polymers known as aromatic polyamides, whose chains consist mainly of rings of carbon atoms linked by atoms of nitrogen.

Theorists studying the electronic bonds between the links of these new polymers believed they could form structures with almost incredible strength, but the temperature required to melt them into usable forms was so high, the molecules disintegrated before the melting point was reached.

The answer to the problem was eventually found by a group of Du Pont chemists, notably Stephanie L. Kwolek, who drew their ideas from the emerging science of liquid crystals.

USE OF LIQUID CRYSTALS

Liquid crystals, one type of which is used in some digital-display watches and calculators, are strange intermediates between true liquids and solid crystals. Water, a true liquid, is a disordered chaos of molecular fragments, while in ice, a true solid, the fragments are arranged in a highly ordered, rigid lattice. There is no intermediate phase between water and ice.

By contrast, certain rodlike polymer molecules can be dissolved in special solvents in such a way that they remain mobile but still influence each other enough to bundle together in highly organized clumps, like logs in a raft. These are liquid crystals.

After decades of research, the Du Pont group discovered a way of preparing aromatic polyamide polymers in the form of liquid crystal solutions — pearly, opalescent liquids nearly as thin as water, which could be forced through the fine holes of the spinning machinery used to make ordinary synthetic fibers. As the solution flows through such holes, its liquid crystals are forced into parallel alignment with each other, interacting to form a strong structure.

The result was a new Du Pont product named Kevlar, which is five times stronger than steel on a weight-for-weight basis. It found immediate use in the reinforcing cord in high-performance tires. Kevlar is also woven into fabric that forms the armor in the latest bulletproof vests.

200 POLICEMEN SAVED

A single layer of Kevlar fabric no thicker than ordinary linen can stop a .38-caliber bullet, and Du Pont officials say that the lives of some 200 policemen were saved in the past year because they wore Kevlar-armored vests. Kevlar-based helmets and flak jackets offering more protection and lighter weight than steel are being made for American soldiers.

Among the fastest growing branches of polymer research is medicine. Since polymers can now be engineered to contain microscopic pores and channels, scientists at the Goodyear Tire and Rubber Company, among many other companies, are devising ways of encapsulating drugs like insulin, which can be implanted near body organs to release their doses over a long period of time.

"For kidney patients," according to Donald V. Hillegass of Goodyear, "researchers are studying a polymer system that could be taken in tablet form to absorb toxins normally processed by kidneys. The polymer and the toxins would be eliminated as solid wastes."

Plastics: Fast Growth Stalls

BY LYDIA CHAVEZ | FEB. 5, 1982

IN THE LAST 10 YEARS, executives in such industries as forest products, steel, tires and oil turned to petrochemicals to get in on the fast-growth business of plastics.

The popularity of plastics, however, has turned into a classic case of too many merchants selling the same wares, and many producers are finding it difficult to make a profit.

The competition moved the Cities Service Company just two weeks ago to write off the cost of a $300 million polyethylene plant that was 20 percent completed. And Dow Chemical has "indefinitely" shelved plans for a new polystyrene plant.

"The plant was postponed because of depressed profits, which are a result of many factors," said Melissa Nettles, a spokesman for Dow, "including the cost of raw materials and the number of competitors."

Petrochemical divisions produce plastic resins made from oil and gas. These resins, or small pellets, are turned into products ranging from garbage bags to cosmetics cases, and also have uses in construction, transportation and medical fields. The most common petrochemicals, and those in oversupply, include polyethylene, polypropylene and polystyrene.

CUTBACK AT UNION CARBIDE

"There is a great deal of excess capacity in polyethylene," said William Joyce, vice president of licensing and technology for a division of the Union Carbide Corporation.

Union Carbide, for example, has had to shut down about 1 billion pounds of capacity since the early 1970's because it became too expensive to operate.

John Peppercorn, a vice president of the Gulf Oil Chemicals Company, said: "We're faced with a situation where we have an enormous oversupply in the petrochemical industry. As a result, pricing has become extremely soft and the profitability atrocious."

The plastics field has encountered not only a crowded marketplace, but also the recession, a dramatic increase in the costs of crude oil, and competition from other products such as glass and lightweight steel. Some producers, attuned to the changes, have developed new technology that has substantially reduced production costs and improved the plastics.

MORE WITHDRAWALS FORESEEN

Analysts and industry executives believe, however, that like Cities Service, other producers will have to drop out before many plastics regain their profitability.

"The plastics industry faces a major shake-out period," said Harry Flavin, an analyst with Merrill Lynch, Pierce, Fenner & Smith in Houston. "Petrochemicals were the glamorous part of the chemical industry and attracted a lot of investment, but a lot of producers failed to realize that the industry was maturing."

Mr. Flavin said that the cutback in expansion by Dow and Cities Service was only the beginning. He compares the oversupply of large volume plastics with that of synthetic fibers in the mid-1970's. Before synthetic fibers recovered, producers cut capacity by 25 percent.

"There is some overcapacity in high-density polyethylene," said Richard G. Askew, president of the Phillips Chemical Company, a subsidiary of Phillips Petroleum. His company recently added 500 million pounds of high-density polyethylene capacity.

"The cancellation of Cities Service's project has removed part of that overcapacity, but there is still some old capacity out," he added. "In all probability the cost of operating the older facilities is creating problems with profit margins." While Phillips does not break out its earnings for specific chemicals, Mr. Askew acknowledged that "we are not making as much money on polyethylene as we used to."

"The bloom is off the rose, there is no doubt about it," added Frank Corbin, director of communications for the Society of the Plastics Industry in reference to many of the high-volume plastics.

COMPETITION IN FIELD SEEN

Howard Kibbel, the plastics society's marketing analyst, said that direct substitution of plastics for steel, glass and other materials will decline. In the future, he said, there will be more "intramaterial" competition with polypropylene competing with other poly plastics.

The decline in the growth of plastics has been sharp. While the demand grew at a rate of five times the gross national product during the mid-1970's, that rate has slowed to one and a half times G.N.P., according to Mr. Flavin.

The competition and higher energy costs have spawned new technology. Union Carbide was one of the first companies to come out with a simplified method of making low-density polyethylene in the late 1970's.

While the advent of such technology leads some analysts to forecast a brighter future for the industry, others believe that the new technology in fact makes it more difficult for producers with the old processes to make a profit.

RECESSION CALLED KEY FACTOR

Fred H. Seimer, an analyst with Smith Barney, Harris Upham & Company, believes that much of the drop in demand can be attributed to the recession and not structural overcapacity. "What's terrible about plastics is the end-use markets," he said. As he sees it, the demand for plastics will return when the economy improves.

However, some of the larger uses for plastics, such as packaging, have not been as affected by the recession as other less important uses, such as transportation. About 28 percent of the plastics sold in the United States are used in packaging, 18 percent in construction, 10 percent in consumer and industrial goods and 7 percent in electrical applications. Only 4 percent are used in the transportation industry.

Gulf's Mr. Peppercorn disagreed: "Even if the economy turns around, I think we're probably faced with an oversupply situation for some time, depending on the particular plastic."

Debate on Safety of Urea Foam and Plastic Tubing

BY PETER KERR | FEB. 25, 1982

THE ANXIETY LEVEL of homeowners may have risen several notches in the last four days, after news reports were published about two synthetic products often found in the home.

On Monday, the Federal Consumer Product Safety Commission banned the sale of urea formaldehyde foam, which has been installed as insulation in hundreds of thousands of houses since the mid-1970's.

Urea formaldehyde has been used mainly to insulate older houses. It is mixed into a foam resembling shaving cream and then pumped into exterior walls, where it hardens.

In a separate matter last weekend, the New York City Transit Authority was criticized for installing plastic electrical tubing made of polyvinyl chloride in subway stations. Yesterday, the Transit Authority said that it would stop installing such tubing but that it would leave the tubing already installed in place.

Polyvinyl chloride is also used in a number of home-related products, including furniture, plumbing systems, electrical wire insulation and conduits.

Some scientists and fire experts contend that polyvinyl chloride products should be limited, particularly in large buildings, because the material can emit deadly and toxic fumes in a fire.

Although the use of both materials has stirred serious and at times passionate debate, the question of their immediate danger to homeowners is still unclear.

In the case of urea formaldehyde, the safety commission urges homeowners not to panic. If such insulation was installed more than a year ago and no residents have experienced health problems, there is probably nothing to worry about, according to Dr. Peter Preuss, associate executive director for health sciences of the safety commission.

"The most frequent signs of health problems caused by urea formaldehyde are eye irritation and irritation of the throat," Dr. Preuss said.

The ban on urea formaldehyde, which takes effect 130 days after the order appears in the Federal Register, was based on research that linked formaldehyde, an ingredient in the insultation, to cancer in animals, but several safety commissioners said that other flu-like illnesses associated with the product were sufficient to call for a prohibition.

The safety commission has logged more than 2,200 consumer complaints of respiratory illnesses and other health problems associated with formaldehyde fumes from the insulation. In cases where the insulation emits formaldehyde fumes, they can seep through gaps in walls or through the walls themselves.

According to the National Insulation Institute, a trade organization that represents installers and manufacturers of the foam, the ban could drive down the value of some of the 500,000 homes in the United States that contain the insulation.

The institute said it plans to attempt to have the ban overturned by Congress and the courts.

"It is really too soon to tell how the ban will affect home values," said Bernard Goodman, a former president of the American Society of Appraisers and the president of Goodman-Marx, a real estate appraisal firm in Mineola, L.I.

"You are dealing with the psychology of buyers," he said. "Maybe it will be like saccharin, where people will eventually say it wasn't as bad as we thought. Or it could be a roadblock to marketability."

People who believe they are experiencing health problems caused by urea formaldehyde foam should first visit a physician, Dr. Preuss said.

The next step, Dr. Preuss said, is to have a chemical laboratory check the house for formaldehyde emissions. If the tests are positive, he suggested contacting the companies that installed and produced the foam.

"Since emissions from formaldehyde decrease with age," Dr. Preuss said, "the risk is quite low in most homes."

According to Dr. Preuss, a contractor can sometimes solve the problem of formaldehyde emissions in a home by simple methods, such as painting, or drilling holes in the outside walls to let the formaldehyde fumes escape. The ultimate step, he said, is to remove the insulation, a step that can cost $10,000 to $20,000.

One problem, said William Fagel, a spokesman for the New York State Health Department, is that few laboratories in the state perform formaldehyde tests in the home.

Jean Cropper, deputy commissioner of the New York City Health Department, said it conducts a limited number of tests on a priority basis.

Homeowners asking questions about the safety of polyvinyl chloride will find themselves in the middle of a battle that includes plastic and steel manufacturers.

In defense of polyvinyl chloride, its producers maintain that their product is no more dangerous in fires than many other building materials. And they argue that the criticisms come primarily from the steel industry, which has an economic interest in cutting the sales of plastics.

"This is an industry battle," said H.F. van der Voort, a spokesman for the Carlon Division of Indian Head Inc., which manufactures polyvinyl chloride pipes, fittings and conduits. "There is no data to suggest that the production of toxic emissions by PVC is worse than other products," he said.

However, several scientists, who say they have no connection with the plastic or steel industries, argue that in fires polyvinyl chloride produces deadly fumes, including hydrogen chloride, at lower temperatures and in greater amounts than other building materials.

"The evidence is lopsided," said Gordon F. Vickery, the former head of the United States Fire Administration, a Federal agency. "In comparison with common materials such as wood, it burns twice as hot, twice as fast, and gives off an incredible amount of toxic gases."

Although it is almost impossible for a consumer to avoid having any polyvinyl chloride products in the home, there are alternatives on the market for certain items — for example, steel conduits and pipes.

Plastic Compound May Be Reviewed

BY MICHAEL DECOURCY HINDS | SEPT. 15, 1983

WASHINGTON, SEPT. 14 — A major inquiry is expected to be authorized Thursday by the Consumer Product Safety Commission into the potential health hazard posed by an animal carcinogen found in most pliable plastic products, including many plastic products used by infants.

The Federal regulatory agency is expected to ask the National Academy of Sciences to review the potential hazard posed by diethylhexyl phthalate, a compound widely used to make plastic pliable. The agency must request an academy review before starting any regulatory action regarding suspected toxins.

In 1982, scientists at the Department of Health and Human Resources found that laboratory animals developed nonfatal liver cancer after being fed what scientists at the Consumer Product Safety Commission said might have been "excessive" amounts of the plasticizing compound. The compound was subsequently listed in a departmental report on substances that are known or reasonably anticipated to be human carcinogens.

The commission is also expected to ask its own staff scientists to begin a sweeping review of the health hazard posed by the compound in children's products, including pacifiers, teething rings, toys, crib bumpers, playpen covers and baby mattresses.

SAFER SUBSTITUTES SOUGHT

The commission hopes its review might also suggest safer substitutes for the phthalate compound. Most pliable plastic products contain up to 40 percent of this compound, according to the commission. These products include flooring, home furnishings, housewares and sporting goods.

Some of the phthalate compound leeches out of the plastic because it does not form a stable chemical bond with the base material, polyvinyl chloride. The compound can be absorbed through the skin or orally, according to the commission. Commission staff also said that the widespread use and disposal of pliable plastic has caused phthalate to exist in very low levels in the general environment.

"We are particularly concerned about the long-term effect on small children since they are literally surrounded by the stuff," said Samuel Zagoria, a member of the commission.

Dr. Peter W. Preuss, director of the commission's health sciences division, said the potential health hazard to children "may range from zero risk to a risk of causing 30 cancers per million people, depending on the risk model used and estimated exposure levels."

Industry gave mixed reviews to the commission's expected vote. Dr. James P. Mieure, chairman of the Chemical Manufacturers Association's panel on phthalates, said it was "premature" for the commission to convene a National Academy of Sciences panel.

Aaron Locker, counsel to the Toy Manufacturers of America, said the commission's expected action was "highly welcome," and added, "There is so much controversy surrounding this subject it makes sense to have the academy take a look at it."

CHAPTER 2

Growing Environmental Concerns

The rapid ascent and dominance of plastics led to environmental concerns later in the 20th century. Plastics are composed of polymers, long chains of repeating hydrocarbon molecules. These large molecules are so close together that they cannot be penetrated by organic matter, thereby stalling decomposition. This problem was met with extensive efforts toward recycling in the 1980s and 1990s. The articles in this chapter illustrate that shift, detail different strategies for breaking down and recycling plastic, and explore attempts at introducing a biodegradable alternative.

Recycling Worries on Plastic Bottles

BY ELIZABETH KOLBERT | AUG. 7, 1986

ON THE SIDE of a can recently tested by the Coca-Cola Company the words "recyclable plastic" are written in bold letters. But the plastic can, which has been test-marketed in Columbus, Ga., has raised concerns among environmentalists and recycling experts.

Many say recycling it will not be economically feasible if it is mass-marketed. Instead, they say, most of the cans will end up in landfills or incinerators, increasing the burden on the nation's overflowing garbage dumps and possibly causing toxic emissions.

The testing of the can has rekindled a debate that began in the late 1970's with the introduction of plastic soda bottles. Plastic bottles now contain about 25 percent by volume of all packaged soft drinks consumed in this country.

Many environmentalists and recycling authorities argue that the increase in plastic containers is being made at the expense of more easily recycled materials — glass and aluminum — and should be countered with legislation. In New Jersey, for example, a proposed bill says that if the recycling of plastic beverage containers does not improve, a deposit might be required.

While calling the test-marketing a success, Coca-Cola has said that it will not use the plastic can until major obstacles to recycling it are overcome, including how to collect used cans. Ron Coleman, speaking for Coca-Cola in Atlanta, said the company had test-marketed the can, which is made in Sweden, "because we like to be in a position to offer our consumers an option." He said consumers found it "appealing."

Environmentalists call Coca-Cola's decision to delay mass-marketing an acknowledgment of the resistance. "I think they were a little surprised by the strength of the opposition," said Jonathan Puth, deposit-law coordinator for Environmental Action, a lobbying group in Washington.

The Kentucky State Senate passed a bill, later killed by the House, that would have effectively banned 12-ounce plastic cans from the state. In New York State, a coalition of environmental groups is seeking to prevent the can from being introduced. "A lot of people see it as a potential threat to continued recycling," said Ivan Braun, an organizer.

Many environmentalists and recycling experts contend that the major obstacle to recycling of plastic is the difficulty of collecting it. Because plastic weighs so little and is worth only a few cents a pound, it is impossible, they say, to amass enough to repay transportation costs.

"The economics of collection are questionable," said Mary Sheil, director of New Jersey's Office of Recycling. While 180 towns in New

Jersey have mandatory recycling of some materials, including glass and aluminum, only two collect plastic, she said.

Another obstacle, some recycling experts say, is the difficulty of separating different types of the material that are often used in the same container. The plastics industry, however, which has established a research institute at Rutgers, the State University of New Jersey, to study ways to improve recycling technology, disputes the belief that plastics cannot readily be reused.

"There is a terrible myth about recycling plastic," said Steve Babinchak, president of St. Jude Polymer of Frackville, Pa., which has a contract with Coca-Cola to recycle the plastic cans from the test market. "Plastic is every bit as recyclable as aluminum."

Unlike glass and aluminum, plastic cannot legally be recycled into new containers because of the dangers of contamination. But recycled plastic can be used in a variety of products, according to plastics manufacturers, ranging from automotive parts to fiberfill for jackets and quilts. Mr. Babinchak said the demand for recycled plastic far outstrips the supply.

According to the National Association of Recycling Industries, an association of scrap dealers, over 50 percent of all aluminum beverage containers were recycled in 1984. The plastics industry has said that in that year, about 20 percent of all plastic bottles were recycled. Comparable figures for glass were not available.

Some experts, such as Jerry Powell, editor of Resource Recycling, a magazine that covers recycling issues, predict that if plastic cans gain wide acceptance, pressure will increase on legislatures to require returnable bottles and cans. "It could tilt the balance so that deposit legislation passes," he said.

Plastic containers that are not recycled are generally dumped in landfills or burned. While most experts on solid wastes say that plastic probably poses no particular problems in landfills, some say they are concerned that a variety of plastics may emit poisonous chemicals when burned.

The plastic can may also encounter opposition from retailers because its shelf life is not as long as a metal can's. "We know there are still a lot of issues to be studied and resolved," said Mr. Coleman of Coca-Cola.

The Environment Versus Plastic

BY RICHARD HAITCH | DEC. 28, 1986

WHEN THE COCA-COLA COMPANY said early this year that it had successfully tested its soft drink in a new plastic can, environmentalists
objected loudly to any full-scale marketing of the container, even
though it was labeled "recyclable plastic."

For about 10 years, environmental groups have watched nervously
as the use of plastic bottles has grown. While in theory plastic can
be recycled, they say, in practice it does not work; plastic weighs so
little and is worth so little that attempts to reclaim it do not even cover
transportation costs, they argue.

Coca-Cola had test-marketed its new can — an aluminum top and
plastic body — in Columbus, Ga. Consumers found it "appealing," a
spokesman reported. But, seemingly taken aback by the strong environmental protests, the company said it would not use the plastic can
until obstacles to recycling it were overcome.

A solution does not appear imminent.

"At this point, everything is under study," says Roy Fleming, the
company's media relations manager in Atlanta. While "the technical people tell me they're making substantial progress," he says, "we
wouldn't really want to make any predictions about it."

Plastics Industry, Under Pressure, Begins to Invest in Recycling

BY MYRA KLOCKENBRINK | AUG. 30, 1988

UNDER PRESSURE FROM anti-pollution legislation and shrinking landfill space, the plastics industry is moving rapidly to develop technology for recycling its products, like beverage bottles and plastic bags, after they have been used by consumers.

Plastics manufacturers are investing research funds, and entrepreneurs are already exploiting existing technologies to draw profits from recycled plastics. Some companies are recovering pure resin polymers from plastic carbonated beverage bottles to create products like fiberfill for pillows, as well as plastic textiles and carpet facing. The industry is also converting mixed and layered types of plastics into plastic lumber for picnic tables and other outdoor uses.

But it is still unclear how much the plastic industry's recent foray into recycling can reduce the burden of waste that is overtaxing the nation's disposal capacities. Critics of the industry question whether recycling will be feasible on a scale large enough to make a difference, and they say that limiting the use of plastics must have the highest priority.

Although the newspaper and aluminum industries began intensive recycling efforts more than 20 years ago, the plastics industry is only now beginning to look at recycling used consumer products. Less than one percent of all plastics are currently recycled, as against 29 percent for aluminum and 21 percent for paper.

BOTTLE LEGISLATION

Separating and collecting reusable plastics from garbage is a major challenge. So far, the industry has primarily relied on legislation in nine states requiring deposits on beverage containers, thus encouraging consumers to return them. But plastic beverage bottles represent only three-tenths of one percent of the plastic produced in the United States.

Environmentalists, on the other hand, say the chief way of eliminating plastic pollution should be reducing the amount and type of plastics produced. "Recycling only takes care of the problem once it's been created," said Jeanne Wirka, a research analyst for the Center for Environmental Education in Washington. She added that plastic production is projected to rise to about 75 billion pounds in the year 2000 from about 50 billion pounds in 1988.

Environmentalists also assert that plastics are too widely dispersed, too mixed in composition and too inexpensive to be profitably recycled. "The very adaptability of plastics is the enemy to recycling efforts," said Barry Commoner, director of the Center for the Biology of Natural Systems at Queens College in New York.

But spokesmen for the plastics industry say the potential for recycling has only begun to be explored. They say markets have been created for recycled plastic products and that once collection technologies improve, new markets will emerge. To ease one of the main problems in recycling — sorting different types of plastics from one another — the Society of the Plastics Industry in Washington recently initiated a voluntary coding system that identifies plastic containers by resin.

ENCOURAGEMENT OF INDUSTRY

Plastic waste, which can take up to four centuries to degrade, contributed 6.8 percent of the weight and 25.4 percent of the volume of the nation's solid wastes in 1984, according to a study by the International Plastics Consultants Corporation of Stamford, Conn.

In addition to recycling, the plastics industry is also working to develop degradable products that would reduce disposal burdens. Although degradable plastics may take over some uses, the interest in recycling remains high. In fact in a reversal of its former opposition, the plastics industry is now urging states and cities to include plastics in their mandatory recycling programs, said Dr. Darrell Morrow, director of the Center for Plastics Recycling Research at Rutgers University.

Legislation aimed at reducing plastic garbage has prompted the research effort. Recently Suffolk County, N.Y., banned the use of polystyrene foam packaging, and about 20 states have proposed bills that would either ban or restrict some plastic packaging.

"No doubt about it, legislation is the single most important reason why we are looking at recycling," said Wayne Pearson, Executive Director of the Plastics Recycling Foundation, a consortium of 45 companies including plastics manufacturers like Du Pont and such beverage manufacturers as Coca-Cola and Pepsi.

PRODUCING NEW PRODUCTS

Inside plastics factories, scrap materials have long been recycled. Only now, though, is technology being used to turn post-consumer plastics from bottles, bags and automotive parts into new products. GE Plastics, a division of General Electric, is studying the possibility of cars with recyclable plastic parts and houses built from recycled plastics.

In the major commercial recycling operation today, 150 million pounds of carbonated beverage bottles are being recycled by six companies in the United States to recover polyethylene terephthalate or PET, a pure plastic resin designed to prevent carbon dioxide in the beverages from leaking out. Wellman Inc. of Johnsonville, S.C., the largest PET recycling company, has been recovering the material since the first bottle bills were passed in Oregon, Iowa and Michigan in 1979. Last year Wellman recycled 100 million pounds of plastic from the 890-million-pound beverage bottle industry into fiberfill and carpet facing.

High-density polyethylene is also being recovered from industrial scrap and from communities with recycling efforts. Though often mixed with other plastics, the recovered material is being turned into a plastic lumber that can be used for fences, picnic tables and highway hardware like sign posts.

SYSTEM DEVELOPED IN EUROPE

Plastic Recycling Inc. of Iowa Falls, Iowa, uses 15,000 pounds of plastics a day to create car stops for parking lots as well as other products.

Three years ago the Plastics Recycling Foundation approached the recycling center at Rutgers University to help industry develop technology for the recycling of plastics packaging. The center studies all aspects of recycling including collection, sorting, reclamation and marketing. But reclamation has attracted the most attention.

In a technique similar to that being used commercially, the center is experimenting with a recycling system developed in Europe to turn mixed plastics into plastic lumber. Ground and dried plastics are drawn through a hydraulically driven extruder, similar to a hand-operated meat grinder, where the plastic melts through internal friction. The melted plastic is forced into a mold on a circular carriage that passes through a water bath to solidify the molded plastic.

The center, unlike most of the companies that use recycled plastics, makes their research available to industry. Until now, most plastics recycling technology has been proprietary, hindering development.

"We have a long way to go," said Dr. Morrow of the Rutgers center. "But plastics recycling has come a long way in a short time. What was once thought of as non-recyclable is now being recycled."

A Second Life for Plastic Cups? Science Turns Them Into Lumber

BY ROBERT HANLEY | **FEB. 22, 1989**

PISCATAWAY, N.J. — A new park bench made of sturdy plastic sits in the hallway of a research office at Rutgers University here, an ornamental testament to a useful second life for the plastic-foam cup and hamburger box.

These cups and boxes, the throw-away staples of the fast-food industry, together with supermarket and school cafeteria trays make up 40 percent of the plastic "lumber" used in the bench. The rest is from plastic bottles, melted and remolded, that once held anti-freeze and detergent, yogurt, liquor and margarine.

For the last year, scientists at the Rutgers Center for Plastics Recycling Research have worked on blending these plastics into planks and posts that someday, they hope, will become an economical substitute for wood in decks, picnic tables, piers and fences.

A RACE AGAINST BANS

The experimental research is something of a race for the center, which is a creation of the plastics industry. Its staff wants to prove that polystyrene — the dominant plastic used in fast-food containers — has value when recycled. The motive is to curb any widening of sentiment among environmentalists and politicians to ban polystyrene from use as a food container.

Technology already exists for recycling the more valuable types of plastics, used in soda bottles and in clear jugs for milk, water and fruit juices.

Before tackling polystyrene, the center helped perfect the machinery that shreds those plastics into flakes, washes and separates them from remnants of bottle caps and paper labels. But recycling of plastics lags far behind newspapers and glass bottles. Widespread use of plastic packaging is only about a decade old, and the public, the industry says, has little awareness that discarded plastic containers are recyclable. As a result, economical methods of collecting and sorting discarded plastics are all but non-existent.

"We can't get anywhere near enough soda bottles," said Dennis Sabourin, vice president of Wellman Inc., the New Jersey-based leader of the plastic-soda bottle recycling industry.

DEPOSIT LAWS IN NINE STATES

Of the 750 million pounds of plastic soda bottles used and thrown away in the country annually, only 150 million pounds, or about 20 percent, are recycled, Mr. Sabourin said. Nearly all come from the nine states that have deposit laws for plastic bottles: New York, Connecticut, Massachusetts, Vermont, Maine, Delaware, Michigan, Oregon and Iowa.

Wellman handles about two-thirds of that volume, he said, transforming the flaked plastic into polyester fiber used in wall-to-wall carpeting, furniture cushions and as insulating fill in comforters and ski jackets.

Besides fibers, chips of soda-bottle plastic, polyethylene terephthalate, more commonly called PET, can be reused to make bathtubs and shower stalls, boat hulls, electrical wall sockets and plastic panels for cars.

Uses for chips of milk-jug plastic, known as high density polyethylene, or HDPE, include toys, trash cans, flower pots, pipes and pails.

ONLY 1% IS RECYCLED

Still, the industry estimates that 99 percent of all discarded plastic containers wind up in landfills, in large measure because only soda bottles and milk jugs have proven new uses. Because the containers are, in essense, bulky plastic bubbles, they use considerable landfill space.

Hence, the value of the research into plastic lumber at the center here.

Ten benches matching the center's hallway ornament were recently shipped from the center to Palm Beach, Fla., the end product of junked plastic packages gathered there last summer in a beach-combing bee.

Piled in the center's workshop are eight-foot plastic planks and posts produced by a Belgian-designed machine that melts plastics to a pudding texture and squeezes it into metal molds.

WILL NAILS POP OUT?

"These are all prototypes. We're still experimenting with a variety of mixes of plastics that scientists once thought were incompatible," said Dr. Thomas J. Nosker, manager of the project.

Questions still unanswered about the "lumber" include its durability and ability to hold fasteners over years. "We have to know that nails won't spit themselves back out," Dr. Nosker said.

"Will there be warping or discoloring?" said Ted Kasternakis, the project's research engineer. "How will the sun change the color? Will there be chipping or cracking? It's all new territory and we have to get a handle on it."

The center was formed in 1985 by the Plastics Recycling Foundation, a non-profit industry organization. It provides 42 percent of the center's $2.3 million budget. New Jersey provides 30 percent, Rutgers, 19 percent, and the rest is from the National Science Foundation and other states.

But even with the center's innovations, officials say, plastics face another recycling hurdle: lightness — the quality that made plastics an economical replacement for glass containers.

Unless systems are created to sort containers by plastic type, compact them, and collect them, the cost of carrying the bulky containers could jeapordize the value scientists may create for recycled products.

For example, discarded plastic soda bottles are worth three times as much as shattered glass bottles. But a standard garbage truck can carry about 30,000 pounds of crushed glass, worth $600, and only about 1,000 pounds of unshredded plastic bottles, worth $60, according to Guy Watson, manager of technical assistance in New Jersey's Office of Recycling.

"That's the crux of the problem to municipal officials," Mr. Watson said. Only 80 of New Jersey's 567 towns recycle plastics, he said.

Degradable Plastics Show Promise in Fight Against Trash

BY WILLIAM K. STEVENS | APRIL 11, 1989

THEY ARE EVERYWHERE: coffee cups and burger boxes, trash and grocery bags, diapers and margarine tubs and containers for everything from milk to antifreeze — billions of pieces of trash, all made of seemingly indestructible plastic.

As the nation's trash crisis builds, some desperate communities are searching for new disposal sites. Others are turning to the recycling of plastics and other waste items. Some are prohibiting plastics outright. Last month, for instance, Minneapolis banned most plastic food packaging from grocery stores and fast-food restaurants until the city can work out an acceptable way to recycle plastics.

But in a sharply different approach, scientists and entrepreneurs, convinced that plastic waste need not be as indestructible as it seems, are coming up with a variety of ways to make plastics that disintegrate over time. Their success is mixed and in some cases preliminary. It has come, however, at a time when plastics are moving to the fore in the quickening national debate over solid-waste disposal. And it has made degradable plastics one of the most talked-about pollution-control technologies.

Such plastics are already on the market in a limited way, most notably in the yokes for beverage six-packs. Not merely unsightly litter, the conventional yokes entangle, injure and kill wildlife. Sixteen states, including New York, New Jersey and Connecticut, now require that they be degradable.

Spurred in part by this success, officials in Washington are promoting degradable plastics, along with recycling, as the wave of the future. Bills aimed at requiring the use of degradable plastics together with recycling have been introduced in Congress, and many states and localities have approved or proposed similar measures.

But in the debate over the issue, scientists, environmentalists and industrialists have all expressed reservations. Some question whether degradables really do degrade as well as claimed. They also wonder about the safety of residues that might be left in the environment by disintegrating plastic.

Even if those questions can be satisfactorily resolved, some fear that degradable plastics might frustrate the recycling of plastic waste, a strategy that some consider more promising. Making plastics degradable, these skeptics say, will make them unfit for recycling.

"People are jumping on this bandwagon," said Ellen Harrison, a spokeswoman for the Waste Management Institute at Cornell University. But, she said, "let's not assume this solves our waste problem; it doesn't."

Few believe that degradables are the final answer, and the degree to which they can be useful hangs largely on fundamental questions of chemistry.

All plastics share an inherent characteristic that is at the root of the degradability problem. Their chemical structure makes them, under most conditions, impervious to disintegration except through oxidation over hundreds of years or through burning.

Plastics are made of polymers, or long chains of repeating hydrocarbon molecules, so tightly bound together that the microscopic fungi and bacteria that dissolve wood and other organic matter cannot penetrate them. This characteristic also gives plastics their strength, and the task for scientists is to weaken the polymers so that they can break apart without sacrificing too much strength.

They attempt to do this in two basic ways. One is to make plastics photodegradable, or vulnerable to breakdown by ultraviolet rays from the sun. The other is to make them biodegradable, or vulnerable to attack by microorganisms.

The photodegradables can be made by mixing light-sensitive chemicals into the plastic resin during production or by incorporating light-sensitive molecules, called carbonyls, into the polymer chains chemically. When exposed to the sun's ultraviolet rays, these chemicals cause the polymers to weaken and break down into shorter units. The plastic becomes brittle and falls apart.

VALUE IN REDUCING LITTER

Packages or containers made of photodegradable plastic do not degrade indoors, since windows block ultraviolet rays. Nor do they degrade if covered up in a landfill.

Experts believe the major value of photodegradables is in reducing litter. Three American companies produce them for beverage yokes, and four others, including one in Canada, are producing them for products like trash bags, grocery bags and plastic film used in agricultural soil to hold nutrients, heat and moisture. Another possible use is in the plastic boxes used to package hamburgers and other fast foods.

"It's very clever stuff," David Wiles, the director of the chemical division of Canada's National Research Council, said in a telephone interview. "Let's go with it. I think it's a real solution."

Dr. Wiles's laboratory, part of a Canadian Government office dealing with standards for materials, has investigated the properties of both kinds of degradable plastics. The research council's counterpart in the United States, the National Institute of Standards and Technology, is just starting to investigate the materials.

Still, some experts say there are better ways to deal with the problem. Ms. Harrison of Cornell said that photodegradable plastic six-pack yokes could take months to disintegrate, depending on climate. "Aren't we better off changing the design in some way?" she said.

POLYMER FROM BACTERIA

The outlook for biodegradable plastics appears less clear than for photodegradables. Some plastics have been produced for medical use — sutures, for example — that break down inside the body. But for other

Farmers have been using plastic coverings to protect crops for years.

uses, biodegradables, with some exceptions, are in the experimental or developmental stages.

In one technique, pioneered by the chemical company ICI Americas Inc., a biodegradable plastic is produced by breeding bacteria normally found in soil. When fed sugar in a fermentation process, the bacteria produce a natural polymer with all the properties of plastic. Filtered and dried, the resin retains its plastic properties in normal use, according to its manufacturers, but degrades under microbial attack when placed in soil, sewage or the ocean floor. It is still under development, but its makers are optimistic about its potential uses.

Another technique for making biodegradable plastic involves adding natural polymers like cornstarch or cellulose to plastic resin to make it vulnerable to microorganisms. A number of variations on this technique have been tried, but applications so far have been limited.

A Canadian company, the St. Lawrence Starch Company, is marketing a plastic to which both cornstarch and an oxidizing agent, simple vegetable oil, have been added. The company says bacteria feed on the cornstarch, exposing more of the material's surface to the oxidizer, which reacts with metal salts in soil to destroy the polymer chains. Eventually, the company says, the fragments become small enough to be eaten by microorganisms. How long that takes depends on factors like heat, moisture and microbial activity, said Peter Campbell, a company engineer.

The company's plastic was introduced in the United States last month in lawn bags manufactured by Petoskey Plastics Inc. of Petoskey, Mich.

HOW MUCH RESIDUE REMAINS?

Other researchers say they have also solved the problem of maintaining the plastic's strength while making it biodegradable. This involves finding the right proportion of starch, or starch and cellulose, and plastic polymer. But there are skeptics. Dr. Wiles, for instance, said that if enough starch were put into a plastic trash bag to cause it to degrade, it would not be strong enough to hold anything, and that if it did hold, it would not fully degrade.

Environmentalists and scientists are concerned not only about how effective all the techniques are, but also about how much residue remains after degradation takes place and whether any toxic substances would be left. The General Accounting Office, an investigative arm of Congress, reported last fall that no standards for such products existed, that very little independent testing had been done, and that definitions of such terms as biodegradable and photodegradable had not yet even been agreed on. Of particular concern, the agency reported, was uncertainty about "the rate of degradation and the safety of the end products."

Environmentalists like Jeanne Wirka, who has studied the problem for the Environmental Action Foundation, a research and advocacy group, fear that toxic ingredients in plastics, like heavy metals used as pigments and stabilizers, would be released by degradation.

But even if degradable plastics are ultimately proved safe and effective, Ms. Wirka said, they might interfere with recycling.

PROCESS IN ITS INFANCY

Recycling, some say, is a potentially more effective strategy. Even naturally biodegradable materials like paper and food do not break down in many landfills because of lack of moisture, oxygen or warmth. Some scientists say it is not unusual to find 20-year-old newspapers in good condition in excavated landfills. Biodegradable plastics, they say, would not degrade any better under the same conditions.

The recycling of plastics is in its infancy. Plastics differ in their molecular structures, and not all can be successfully melted down and recast. And coloring dyes, once in the plastic, cannot be removed.

A recycling center in Santa Monica, Calif. Methods of collection vary between different cities and states.

About 20 percent of all plastic beverage bottles are now recycled, but only 1 percent of all plastics is recycled.

One problem, Ms. Wirka said, is that degradable plastics and recyclable plastics "in many ways are competitors."

"Recyclers consider the additives to be contaminants," she said.

"It's a really mixed picture," said Howard Levenson, a senior analyst at the Congressional Office of Technology Assessment, who is working on a study on solid waste. "Everywhere we've turned it comes up, yes, there are problems. But there are problems with everything else, too."

Local Laws Take Aim
at Indestructible Trash

BY WILLIAM E. SCHMIDT | APRIL 23, 1989

IN THE EARLY 1980'S, the cities of St. Paul and Minneapolis joined a growing number of cities and counties with curbside recycling programs,
picking up glass bottles, aluminum cans and newspapers that might
otherwise go into landfills or incinerators.

But officials in the Twin Cities noticed that more and more of the
stuff people were throwing out included things like milk jugs, soft
drink containers, grocery bags and egg cartons that used to consist of
paper or cardboard or glass, but now were made out of various plastics
that the city could not recycle.

Now the officials, in a move likely to be imitated elsewhere, are insti-
tuting the most far-reaching waste-management measures yet: ordinances aimed at banning from store shelves and fast-food restaurants
any plastic carry-out food packaging that cannot be recycled. The Minneapolis City Council unanimously adopted the ordinance, which takes
effect in July 1990, at the end of March; St. Paul is expected to pass its
version this month. The two ordinances reflect the urgency with which
many local governments across the country are approaching the issue
of solid-waste disposal, amid growing concern about shrinking landfill
space and the potential environmental consequences of incineration.

E.P.A. PROJECTIONS

"Solid waste disposal is almost wholly a local concern," said Jeanne
Wirka, an analyst with the Environmental Action Foundations in Washington. "People can't necessarily do anything about the Alaska oil spill,
but they can do something about recycling and plastics," she said.

The Environmental Protection Agency predicts that plastic products, which now make up about 7 percent of the waste stream, will
account for 15 percent by the year 2002.

Food manufacturers and retailers say the switch to plastic packaging, which is now commonly used in everything from ketchup bottles to the foam pads inside packaged meats, is a boon to consumers, being lighter and more economical than glass or paper alternatives.

But in the Twin Cities, public officials see it another way. "It's crazy," said Bob Long, a member of the St. Paul City Council who sponsored the ordinance. "As a matter of public policy, we are trying to recycle more and more of our garbage. And the food industry is packaging more and more foodstuffs in plastic that we can't recycle."

SUFFOLK COUNTY'S MOVE

The involvement of local governments with solid-waste disposal began with a growing interest in public recycling efforts. Since 1986, states including New Jersey, Rhode Island and Oregon, have adopted recycling programs, and New York City will start pickups of bottles, cans and newspapers this year.

Now some cities are taking on plastics as a kind of symbolic next step. Both Berkeley, Calif., and Suffolk County passed bans last year on the use of polystyrene plastic for fast foods or other foods packaged by local retailers. The Suffolk County law, which is due to take effect in July, is the object of a lawsuit filed by plastic manufacturers.

Within the last few weeks, hundreds of cities and organizations have asked Minneapolis for copies of its new ordinance, and a statewide version of the law was introduced in the Minnesota Legislature two weeks ago. It would ban all manner of plastic containers, with provisions to exempt products whose manufacturers can prove they can be recycled.

In Minnesota, food retailers and plastic manufacturers are urging the state lawmakers to effectively pre-empt the Minneapolis and St. Paul laws. Failing that, the industry plans to go to court. Still, the threat of more curbs on plastics has had an effect on the industry. There is increasing talk about developing degradable plastics, and several large companies have invested $1.8 million in research aimed at developing new ways to recycle their products.

While about 29 percent of aluminum and 21 percent of paper is currently recyclable, less than 1 percent of plastic goods are recycled, mostly as fiberfill for pillows or carpet facing.

Susan Vadney of the Society of the Plastic Industry says plastics can be 100 percent recyclable, and argues that the principal effect of laws banning them is to drive up grocery prices because paper and glass are more expensive.

In Minneapolis and St. Paul, officials say they cannot afford to recycle plastics because the scrap value of such items is far less than the cost of collecting them. If the industry is serious about recycling, said Mr. Long, the solution is simple: They should subsidize local recycling programs.

Doubts Are Voiced on 'Degradable' Plastic Waste

BY JOHN HOLUSHA | OCT. 25, 1989

AN INNOVATIVE AND widely promoted effort to sell plastic products that are "degradable" could be causing more environmental problems than it is solving.

The very ingredients added to make a plastic break down can make it less fit for recycling programs that are far more beneficial, say environmental groups, researchers and some major plastics producers. They also say that many degradable products have little value because disintegration takes place slowly in the oxygen-starved, dry environment of modern landfills. And they note that it is unclear whether the plastic breaks down into elements that are any less harmful than the plastic itself.

What is more, they say that such products may divert people from participating in fledgling plastic-recycling efforts and encouraging the creation of better recycling technologies and broader programs. Recycling of plastic is far less common than that of aluminum and glass.

"These plastics are being sold as a way to reduce waste and that is a hoax," said Jeanne Wirka, an official of the Environmental Action Foundation, based in Washington, which studies environmental issues. "The notion is that these things will go away, but very little happens to waste that is entombed in a landfill."

"Degradable is a warm and fuzzy word, like organic and natural," said Richard A. Denison, a senior scientist at the Environmental Defense Fund, which is based in New York. "The concern is that if people think you can toss plastic away and it magically disappears, they will just toss it away."

Manufacturers in some industries have moved swiftly toward degradable plastic products to reach people worried about the environment and respond to hundreds of legislative proposals nationwide to ban or restrict such goods. Degradable plastic products, which are supposed to break down into their basic components more quickly, now include trash bags, disposable diapers, six-pack rings and sheets used on farms to hold down weeds. What is more, proponents of degradable products have been moving in recent months to promote their use in a broad variety of plastic packaging.

The Archer-Daniels-Midland Company, for example, raised the anger of environmental groups earlier this year by showing a television commercial that suggested a bin full of plastic containers would simply fade away if treated with the company's biodegrading agents.

Many of the products are now packaged to emphasize degradability. On boxes of Hefty trash bags, for example, an eagle soars over a tree with the headline word "Degradable," and text on the back says the bags represent "a step in our commitment to a better environment."

The makers of degradable plastic products argue that they help make roadside litter disappear more quickly and certainly cannot hurt in landfills.

The debate comes as the popularity of plastic products, particularly for consumer goods, continues to grow. In a new report on the use of plastics and waste disposal, the Environmental Action Coalition, a New York-based group, estimated that plastics would constitute 10 percent of municipal solid waste by the end of the century, compared with about 3 percent in 1970. In a survey of supermarkets, it found that 50 percent of all items were packaged entirely in plastic.

And plastic containers are a disproportionately large disposal problem because of the space they take up in landfills. Estimates are that plastics consume 30 percent of landfill space.

Plastics-industry officials say the very qualities that have made the materials popular in packaging — light weight, strength and inertness — work against them once a package has been used. A plastic box that held a hamburger for a few minutes can foul the environment for decades after being thrown by the roadside.

"Plastics are 7 percent of the solid waste stream by weight, 30 percent by volume and 40 to 50 percent of the litter," said Anthony E. Redpath, an official of Ecoplastics Ltd., speaking at a recent plastics conference in New York. He noted that in the past the visibility of bottles and cans discarded along roadways caused them to be singled out for new laws requiring deposit-and-return programs, and suggested that plastics might be subject to similar treatment.

Plastics-industry officials say that more than 350 legislative initiatives have been introduced at the Federal, state and local levels in the last year to curb the use of products like foam hamburger boxes.

Degradability means that a material decomposes into basic constituents like water and carbon dioxide through some natural process. Because all complex materials will eventually degrade, the term is usually applied to products that have been treated to accelerate breakdown.

There are two major types of degradable plastic materials. Both operate by breaking down the very long chain molecules that give polymeric plastics their strength.

Photodegradable materials break down because of the effect of ultraviolet radiation on chemicals that have been blended with the basic plastic resin. Photodegradable products include Hefty and similar trash bags and the plastic rings that hold six-packs of cans.

Biodegradable plastics are susceptible to attack by microorganisms in the soil through an added organic material, usually corn starch. Biodegradable bags and disposable diapers are available in some areas. Because biodegradables represent a new market for corn products, farm groups and food processors like Archer-Daniels-Midland have been pressing their merits.

But the plastics industry has said it prefers recycling as the way to reduce waste.

"Degradable plastic is inherently a less valuable material," said Karl Kamena, an official of the Dow Chemical Company, a plastic maker. He said products made from recycled degradable plastic were likely to be weaker and performed less well than those made from virgin chemicals. Most of the major plastics producers have joined an industry group, the Council for Solid Waste Solutions, to promote recycling.

"Degradability could put a silver bullet in the heart of recycling," said Dr. Daryl Ditz, a researcher at the Cornell Waste Management Institute. "You don't want recycled products breaking down."

Plastics are more difficult to recycle than aluminum or glass because they come in a variety of chemical formulations. Under the threat of legislative bans, however, plastics producers have begun to sponsor efforts to sort and recycle some products.

But degradable products are appealing because they appear to offer an easy way out for the public, Mr. Kamena said. "Degradability sounds better than recycling because people do not have to do anything," he said. "It puts all the responsibility on the manufacturer."

Producers of degradable products defend them as at least a partial answer to garbage and litter problems. "Is it a perfect solution? No," said Rajeev Bal, the president of Webster Industries, which makes Good Sense photodegradable shopping and trash bags. "But it is better than no solution."

Proponents of degradability say the plastic producers simply fear losing part of their market as products that used to be pure plastic are diluted with nonplastic materials like corn starch. "We can replace 6 percent of plastic" in thin sheets used in bags "and up to 20 percent in polystyrene," said Jerry L. Petak, an official of Archer-Daniels-Midland. "No plastic producer will stand for losing 6 to 20 percent of his market."

Experts on landfills say the degradability feature could help dispose of roadside litter but has little value in modern landfills because disintegration takes place so slowly. Indeed, officials of the Mobil Corporation, which makes Hefty bags, concede that the bags' degradability will do little to solve the environmental problem of garbage disposal, because most will be buried in landfills soon after use. But they say many customers want them anyway.

"They may be some help with the litter problem but they are no help with solid waste," said Allen Gray, a Mobil spokesman. He added, however, that competing brands had been using degradability to increase sales. "We are putting them out there because that is what people are buying right now," he said.

Most environmentalists favor recycling over degradation, although at the same time many deplore the shift to plastic containers from glass and aluminum, which are already heavily recycled.

One important issue concerning degradability, environmentalists say, is just what used plastics degrade into. Biodegradable products based on starch wind up as plastic dust after microorganisms eat the starch. "I consider this to be a consumer scam," said Nancy A. Wolf, executive director of the Environmental Action Coalition. "People think it becomes soil, but it does not. You end up with shards of plastic."

What happens to the little pieces of plastic is not well understood, researchers say. "We have no good answers," said Dr. Ditz of Cornell. "As the molecules become smaller, they become more mobile. They may migrate or become volatile." Other potential dangers of all plastics, environmentalists say, are the release of chemicals used in their preparation, and the escape of toxic coloring agents once the plastic starts to break down.

In Its Latest Recycling Effort, Staten Island Targets Plastic

BY ALLAN R. GOLD | SEPT. 11, 1990

STATEN ISLAND RESIDENTS yesterday began separating most kinds of plastic from their garbage, in the latest expansion of New York City's mandatory recycling program.

The new effort makes Staten Island the first borough to separate six recyclable materials, which will eventually be required in all areas under the city's 17-month-old recycling law. Staten Island residents already bundle newspapers, magazines and corrugated cardboard, and place metal and glass in city-provided containers for curbside pickup.

Plastic products and packaging make up a growing part of municipal waste. The Federal Government estimates that such trash will increase by 50 percent in the next 10 years. Many recycling programs across the nation already include separation of plastic from household garbage, and recycling markets for several kinds of plastic are being developed.

The Sanitation Department, which operates the recycling program, has been gradually expanding the list of items that residents must separate, and has been increasing the number of neighborhoods that must begin sorting some materials from household garbage.

QUEENS AND BROOKLYN NEXT

Mandatory recycling has reached 27 of the city's 59 community districts, or 1.7 million of its 3 million households. This fall, selected districts in Queens and Brooklyn will join Staten Island in mandatory plastic separation, including Bayside, Jamaica, Forest Hills, Park Slope, Carroll Gardens and Cobble Hill.

More than 1,100 tons of recyclable material is now collected each day, the Sanitation Department says, which represents about 6 percent of all trash that city trucks pick up from residences. The recycling law calls for recycling 25 percent of the city's waste by the end of 1994.

In the new phase of the program, the Sanitation Department will collect rigid plastic like milk jugs and laundry detergent bottles. Residents are required to separate the plastic from other household garbage and place it, along with metal and glass, in the blue curbside recycling containers provided by the city.

Plastic, metal and glass collected on Staten Island will be taken to a privately owned processing center in Newark for sorting and eventual sale to recyclers.

NO FILM OR FOAM

Other plastic items acceptable for recycling are soft-drink containers, yogurt and sour-cream containers, clear take-out salad-bar trays and old toys with all nonplastic parts removed.

The Sanitation Department will not collect film plastic, like grocery bags and dry-cleaning covers, or polystyrene foam. Film plastic is difficult to keep free of contamination, an essential condition for recyclers.

The Sanitation Department has hesitated to include polystyrene foam, used for cups and plates, in the recycling program because the City Council may eventually limit its use. In any case, recycling efforts for foam are still in the early stages.

COOPERATIVE RESIDENTS

Staten Island's 135,000 households have been among the city's most cooperative recyclers, said Anne Canty, a Sanitation Department spokeswoman. By April 1989, when the recycling law was passed by the City Council, a voluntary program to separate newspapers, metal and glass for curbside pickup was already in place there.

Two explanations are offered for Staten Island's strong compliance record. First, it has a high percentage of residents who live in single-family homes, which lend themselves to recycling programs because there is more room for storage.

Also, Staten Island residents are more aware of the city's big garbage disposal problem because the giant Fresh Kills Landfill there is considered an environmental blight, borough and Sanitation Department officials say.

A Setback for Polystyrene

BY JOHN HOLUSHA | NOV. 18, 1990

MANUFACTURERS OF POLYSTYRENE, the lightweight plastic packaging material, have been struggling for two years to improve their environmental image by establishing a recycling program. But all of their efforts may have been undone by the decision earlier this month by the McDonald's Corporation to switch from plastic foam to paper packaging for its hamburgers.

Leaders of the polystyrene recycling effort, which is backed by some of the biggest petrochemical companies in the nation, vow they will press on despite the defection of McDonald's. The fast-food chain, the biggest in the nation, was the most prominent participant in pilot recycling programs based in New York and Massachusetts and was to have been part of a planned nationwide program.

"What McDonald's did was give us another quarter of red ink," said Russ Welton, vice president of the National Polystyrene Recycling Company, which is building four recycling plants across the country. Without McDonald's, company executives are scrambling to line up school and industrial cafeterias, big users of foam cups and plates, as new sources of supply.

But some industry observers say the switch by McDonald's will have much bigger repercussions for the $2.5 billion industry.

"Food manufacturers will think twice about continuing to use polystyrene and other plastic packaging," said Peter Coombes, the editor of Chemical Week magazine.

"McDonald's was the engine driving this program," said Nancy Wolf, executive director of the Environmental Action Coalition in New York. "Without them, the whole polystyrene recycling system may collapse."

Some environmentalists have questioned the value of the recycling effort, saying it puts a mantle of respectability on a material whose manufacture generates pollution and which is particularly troublesome as litter. They say the foam is so light it is difficult to collect and transport economically. And they argue that if the chemical industry withdraws the subsidies it has used to start recycling, the effort may end.

"THUS FAR, polystyrene recycling is more a problem-ridden theory than a proven option," said Frederic D. Krupp, executive director of the Environmental Defense Fund, which is helping McDonald's improve its environmental performance and influenced the company's decision to drop the foam box. "There is a lot of pressure on the companies that make polystyrene to say they are recycling, but saying it does not mean it will really happen."

Mr. Krupp noted that the recycling program does not even address the approximately 50 percent of the packaging that leaves fast-food restaurants with takeout orders.

Leaders of the foam recycling effort concede that early efforts to re-use the material have not been profitable and have been hampered by contamination with paper and food waste. But they say four new, much larger plants in the Chicago, Philadelphia, Oakland, Calif., and Los Angeles areas will be able to stand on their own financially.

"Startups always lose money initially," said Mr. Welton of National Polystyrene. "But we are not saying to the industry, 'Subsidize us for 10 years.' I think we can get to a positive cash flow by the end of 1991."

The polystyrene industry began the recycling effort late in 1988 after some areas, including Suffolk County on Long Island, banned the material as part of their response to the solid-waste crisis. Although foam plastic is a small part of all solid waste, hamburger boxes have been singled out by environmental groups because of their very short useful life and prominence as litter.

However, most of these bans include exceptions for materials that are, or can be, recycled. To keep the enacted bans from taking effect, as well as to deter new ones, the polystyrene producers must keep the recycling program alive.

In November 1988, Mobil Chemical and the Genpak Corporation set up a recycling operation in Leominster, Mass., called Plastics Again, which has since been absorbed by National Polystyrene. Early last year, the Amoco Foam Products Company established Polystyrene Recycling Inc. in the Greenpoint section of Brooklyn in association with McDonald's.

Since then, the industry has united behind National Polystyrene and pledged to recycle 250 million pounds of the material by 1995. Company executives said this represents about one-quarter of the billion pounds of plastic foam used in various food packaging applications, and thus is responsive to the Environmental Protection Agency's goal of reaching a 25 percent recycling goal by that date.

The companies that each put up $2 million last fall to start National Polystyrene are Amoco Chemical, Arco Chemical, Chevron Chemical, Dow Chemical, Fina Oil and Chemical, Huntsman Chemical, Mobil Chemical and Polysar.

But the amount to be recycled is a small fraction of the more than 5 billion pounds of polystyrene used in this country each year. Sometimes referred to by the Dow Chemical trade name Styrofoam, polystyrene is also used as molded packaging blocks for shipment of electronic devices, loose packing materials and in the construction and home furnishing industries. Most of these products end up in landfills, where they break down very slowly. But a huge amount simply becomes litter.

"WHEN WE DID a cleanup of the Merrimack River, the biggest single item we found was Styrofoam," said Pat Scanlan, the director of recycling at Wheelabrator Technologies Inc., recounting a cleanup effort he was part of in Massachusetts with a group of friends. "A lot of it was packaging. People threw boxes in the river after buying appliances. The cardboard dissolved, but the Styrofoam floated on to the shore."

Foam plastic's light weight is the major obstacle to recycling, environmentalists and industry executives agree. Although re-using the material simply involves remelting and forming into a new shape, the obstacles posed by collection, shipment and decontamination remain formidable.

"The people who run curbside collection programs don't want to have anything to do with it," Mr. Scanlan said. "They are paid by the ton of material delivered, but the polystyrene takes up space without adding much weight."

"The big cost is transportation," said Tom Tomaszek, the former manager of the Plastics Again plant who now heads a plastics recycling company in Fort Edward, N.Y. "You have to go after other materials in addition to polystyrene to get favorable economics."

Ollie Ligon, an executive at Amoco Foam Products and president of the Brooklyn operation, conceded that "the cost of collection and processing exceeded the value of the resin." The Brooklyn plant paid nothing for the material it received; the shippers benefited by not having to pay the cost of disposal.

MR. WELTON SAID new methods of compressing the foam are being developed, allowing economical truckloads. But the manager of a recycling program in Fitchburg, Wis., said it took all night in a baling machine to compress 275 pounds of foam. A bale made quickly, she noted, only weighs 75 pounds.

In addition, foam that has been used in connection with food has to be washed before it can be remelted, or the resulting contamination will weaken the mechanical properties of the plastic. Executives at National Polystyrene said McDonald's was unable to persuade its customers to separate the plastic foam hamburger boxes from paper wrappings and food waste. As a result, the material arrived at the Leominster facility heavily contaminated and yielded low-quality plastic.

For that reason, Rubbermaid Inc., which said it was eager to use recycled plastic in its household and office products, has only accepted one shipment that was remelted at Plastics Again. "The quality of the material we were getting from McDonald's was terrible," said Mr. Welton of National Polystyrene, the current owner of Plastics Again. "And the material we were producing at the plant was not sufficient to meet the needs of customers like Rubbermaid."

Charles J. Lancelot, materials manager for Rubbermaid Commercial Products, said the company had used only "modest" amounts of recycled plastic foam. But he said Rubbermaid was prepared to use more "if it is consistently available in the right quantity and quality."

Mr. Welton said the new plants, the first of which will open later this year in the Los Angeles area, will each be capable of recycling 13 million pounds of plastic a year, compared with 3 million at Leominster. "At 2 to 3 million, I'm marginal," he said. "At 13 million, I can be profitable."

But McDonald's isn't the only fast-food chain to turn away from foam. Burger King, the second-biggest chain, has used paper-based packaging all along except for coffee cups, which it plans to replace as well. Other chains say they may soon follow suit.

To make up for the loss, the polystyrene recyclers say they are focusing on school and industrial cafeterias. Schools, they note, do not have the carryout problem of fast-food restaurants and students are more dutiful in separating foam trays from other wastes.

National Polystyrene has signed up the Los Angeles school system, and executives say this is typical of the types of supply arrangements the company will use to replace McDonald's. The company's plant in Corona, Calif., will pay 4 cents a pound for foam delivered to its doors.

Beth Lauargand, a business manager for the school system, said it already hauls its own garbage, so it has trucks and a collection system in place. Recycling the foam, she said, "would be very difficult to do unless you are fortunate enough to be in our circumstances."

Pepsi and Coke to Offer Recycled-Plastic Bottles

BY BARNABY J. FEDER | DEC. 5, 1990

COKE AND PEPSI took their long rivalry to the environmental arena yesterday, with each company saying it would be the first to sell soft drinks in plastic bottles made with materials recycled from used bottles.

The recycling programs are set to begin next year and if successful might eventually reduce the amount of the plastic that ends up in the nation's landfills. They might also encourage more communities to set up recycling programs, by putting more cash in the pockets of companies that collect recyclable material. Both companies said recycling would not affect the cost of their products.

The Coca-Cola Company and its supplier, Hoechst Celanese Fibers Inc., have already applied to the Food and Drug Administration for approval of their new bottle, which will have about 25 percent recycled material. Goodyear Tire and Rubber, the supplier of the recycled material in the Pepsi bottle, said it expected to meet with the Federal agency in the spring to seek approval. Both companies said they would test-market the bottles once they had approval before trying to use them nationwide.

CONSUMER ENTHUSIASM

Even if consumers are enthusiastic or at least neutral when it comes to buying recycled bottles, the programs may never account for a large percentage of the companies' output unless consumers become more reliable about returning the bottles after they have slaked their thirst.

Polyethylene terephthalate, or PET, the material used in the bottles, is already recycled by a number of manufacturers into products ranging from park benches and piping to carpet and bedding. They are using everything they can get their hands on — the equivalent of 1.2 billion two-liter bottles, or 28 percent of PET output last year, according to estimates.

Unless Coke, Pepsi and the chemical companies working with them can substantially lift the number of bottles being recycled, they will simply be competing with the existing recyclers for the currently limited pool. And some experts say they will find that extremely costly.

'PUBLIC RELATIONS EXERCISE'

"I think this must be a public relations exercise," said Thomas M. Duff, president and chief executive of Wellman Inc., the nation's largest independent plastics recycler. "They've lost track of the economics." Mr. Duff said products like carpets were more valuable than bottles, so that soft-drink companies would be outbid for the used PET if supplies were limited. The soft-drink companies argue that their recycling programs are more environmentally sound because reusing the material from bottles to make bottles — known as "closing the loop" — keeps the PET out of landfills indefinitely.

Nevertheless, they are trying to avoid a confrontation with other recyclers by encouraging a surge in supplies. Their preferred approach is to sharply expand curbside recycling.

Leaders of Plastics Industry Seeking 25% Recycling Goal

BY JOHN HOLUSHA | MARCH 29, 1991

WASHINGTON, MARCH 28 — Perceiving a strong public demand for environmentally sound products, leaders of the plastics industry said today that they would seek to recycle 25 percent of all plastic bottles and containers produced every year by 1995.

The most recent figures from the Environmental Protection Agency show that only slightly more than 1 percent of all plastic products are currently recycled.

John E. Pepper, the president of Procter & Gamble, one of the largest users of plastic packaging, cited "a real sea change" in environmental concerns in the last several years. "I have never seen an issue change with such force," he added.

The Society of Plastic Industries said legislation to curb the use of plastic packages was pending at some level in 49 states.

Mr. Pepper and Edgar S. Woolard Jr., the chairman of the Du Pont Company, said plastics producers and users would spend $20 million a year through their trade group, the Council for Solid Waste Solutions, to help promote plastics recycling.

They said the assistance would take the form of information for communities seeking to recycle; matching collectors with processors, and buying recycled plastic to use in new products.

About 1,500 municipalities in this country operate curbside recycling programs, one-third of which include plastics.

Mr. Pepper said people believe that plastics are hostile to the environment, even though paper and paper products constitute a far larger component of trash.

"Plastics is the new kid on the block," he said. "They are made of chemicals by oil companies, so they cannot be good for the environment." Yet, he said, many of the most popular types of plastics can easily be recycled if they are collected.

According to officials of the council, which held today's news conference, the capacity to reprocess plastics has been growing faster than plastic collection. They said the 900 companies in the business were running at only 66 percent of capacity.

This is in contrast to old newspapers, which quickly produced a glut a few years ago in the Northeast when many communities began collection programs. The reason was the lack of capacity to process them into new products, a situation that has improved.

Separating Plastic Wheat and Chaff

BY JOHN HOLUSHA | JUNE 2, 1991

PISCATAWAY, N.J. — Plastic bottles rush along a conveyor belt here at Rutgers University's Center for Plastic Recycling Research. They are a diverse mix: clear, green, translucent, opaque; some are intact, some partially crushed.

As they whiz along at 150 to 200 feet per second, they pass between light sources and sensors. Blasts of compressed air blow the bottles off the line into the appropriate bins. The line is sorting the containers by chemical type and color, with a goal of producing materials with more value than the mixed varieties used to make things like plastic lumber.

Finding a way to sort mixed materials quickly and accurately may be the key to making plastics recycling practical. Unlike aluminum cans, which are of uniform composition, plastics come in a variety of colors and chemical formulations, called resins.

The chemical industry is eager to demonstrate that plastics are recyclable, because legislation restricting or taxing plastic products is pending in most states.

Two industry giants, the Du Pont Company and Waste Management Inc., have formed a joint venture, the Plastic Recycling Alliance, to demonstrate that soda bottles made of polyethylene terephthalate and milk bottles made of high-density polyethylene can be commercially recycled.

But at one recent conference on plastics, Jane Witheridge, Waste Management's vice president for recycling, said the project "is not working for us." Because manufacturers have been unwilling to take back many types of plastic, recycling is "not now economically sustainable," she said.

Officials of the Council for Solid Waste Solution, a plastic industry trade association concentrating on recycling, said sorting is the main problem. "The people who buy recycled plastics require a quality sort," said Jean Statler, a council official. "If they are buying blue bottles, they want blue, not orange or red. The markets are there if the materials are sorted by color."

Now, most sorting is done by hand. Workers stand next to a conveyor and try to identify the different types of plastic and toss them into the right bins. Color is simple; beyond that, it can be difficult.

For example, most clear bottles are made of polyethylene terephthalate, generally known as PET. But some of the clear containers — a small percentage — are made of polyvinyl chloride. The only way to tell the difference is to look at the code number on the bottom of the bottle. PET is 1; PVC is 3.

The problem is that PVC can contaminate PET. PVC melts at a lower temperature than PET, so when the PET is processed, the PVC burns, mixing black particles in the clear plastic. "One PVC bottle in a bale can spoil the whole load," said Jose R. Fernandes, a project manager at the Rutgers center.

That is why the first detector on the line looks for PVC. Unlike PET, each molecule of PVC contains a chlorine atom. This causes it to fluoresce, or glow, when subjected to X-ray radiation.

The detector emits a low-powered X-ray beam at the bottles passing by. If it detects a glow (invisible to the human eye), a valve opens and a blast of air with a pressure of 80 pounds per square inch blows the bottle off the line and into a bin.

Optical detectors continue the separation. Light shining through clear bottles activates the air blast. A more intense light detects transparent green, and one that is still more intense separates translucent milk bottles. Other types, mostly opaque colored bottles, run off the end of the line into a container.

Mr. Fernandes and his colleagues have been debugging the line for nine months. One problem concerns the random orientation of the bottles on the line. Looking through the handle of a bottle, a detector might falsely conclude it is transparent. The answer was to add a detector on top of the line, as well as alongside it.

Another problem involves labels and dissimilar materials. Encountering a heavily printed paper label or a solidly colored base on a soda bottle, the detectors might conclude the bottle is opaque. So the detectors have now been programmed to act on the most intense transmission of light through a container. Thus, the transparent part of a bottle, not other sections, would trigger the air blast.

Once they are separated by resin and color, the bottles are ready to be recycled. Paper labels, polypropylene labels and aluminum caps, as well as residual soda and milk are contaminants to plastic and must be removed.

The bottles are chopped into flakes about one-quarter-inch square and washed with hot water and industrial detergent. This cleans off the milk and soda and reduces the paper to a fine pulp that is carried off with the wash water and filtered out.

An electrostatic precipitator pulls out most of the aluminum shreds. The plastic and remaining metal are poured onto a rotating drum and subject to 12,000 volts of static electric charge. The metal, being a good conductor of electricity, falls off the drum. The plastic, a poor conductor, sticks until the charge is canceled.

The plastic flakes are run through a cone-shaped piece of equipment where swirling water separates the lighter, high-density polyethylene from the heavier PET. The flakes are dried and loaded in large cardboard boxes for shipment to plastics users.

The current system represents first-generation technology, Mr. Fernandes said. Under development is another system that would group all the detectors in one location. As a bottle came past the detection station, the identification would be loaded into a computer's memory, which would assign a gate where each bottle would be blown off. Knowing the rate of movement of the conveyor, computer-managed relays then would activate the air blast when the bottle reached the appropriate gate.

Other detectors could be added as well. Since each type of resin has its own infrared "fingerprint," infrared detectors could separate different types of plastic.

Turning Waste Plastics Into Fuels

BY JOHN HOLUSHA | AUG. 28, 1991

WARREN, MICH. — As complex plastics increasingly replace metals in cars and appliances, recycling these products becomes a larger problem. Attention is now turning to a high-temperature process called pyrolysis that breaks down plastics into burnable oil and gas.

Auto makers and plastic suppliers hope to demonstrate within a few years that this technique has great commercial potential. Environmental advocates question whether pyrolysis is truly recycling, but backers of the technique say it is far better than throwing the plastic away.

Pyrolysis breaks materials down by heating them at high temperatures in the absence of air. Because no oxygen is present, plastics and rubber left over from cars do not burn, as they would in an incinerator. Instead, the heat, about 1,300 degrees Fahrenheit, breaks the complex hydrocarbons down into simpler molecules, producing a liquid resembling heating oil and a combustible gas, along with some ash.

POTENTIAL FOR POLLUTION

Because nothing except the fuel for the pyrolysis reactor is burned, the technique may cause less air pollution than incinerators. But if the gas produced by pyrolysis is used to heat the reactor once it reaches operating temperature, as most plans envision, pollution will result from plastic and rubber that contain chlorine or sulfur, said Raymond Machacek, of A. D. Little, a consulting firm.

Vinyl plastics contain chlorine, and sulfur is used in the vulcanization of rubber. The chlorine and sulfur atoms tend to form hydrochloric and sulfuric acids, which are toxic pollutants, Mr. Machacek said.

The growing amount of plastic in automobiles causes grumbling among metal recyclers, because it results in more worthless material that must be disposed of in landfills, at additional cost. Unlike plastic soda bottles, which can easily be reprocessed, most of the plastics left after cars are shredded and the metals extracted are composites of materials that have been further contaminated by paint and adhesives.

"Very often you will have incompatible plastics glued together," said Richard L. Klimisch, an environmental specialist at the General Motors Corporation's Technical Center here. In addition, many of the plastics are a type known as thermosets, which cannot be melted down and used again, like the material in soda bottles.

A car on exhibit at the technical center, cut away to display new sound-deadening insulation materials, also inadvertently illustrates how difficult these new materials might be to recycle. Several of the insulating materials are simply labeled, "Complex blend of various stuff."

Researchers at the G.M. Technical Center are running perhaps the largest pyrolysis trials, but an association that includes several major plastic and rubber makers, including Goodyear Tire and Rubber, Dow Chemical, Eagle-Picher, Allied-Signal and Owens-Corning Fiberglas, is also experimenting with the technique.

Industry trends make it clear that metal recyclers are going to have to find ways to cope with more plastic. "Cost is driving the industry to greater use of plastic," said Irvin E. Poston, a plastics specialist at G.M.

He notes that plastic body parts are lighter than steel, requiring less costly tooling to shape and improving fuel economy. The entire outer body of G.M.'s new line of mini-vans, like the Chevrolet Lumina APV, is made of composite plastic. Pyrolysis recovers the energy content of plastic after its useful life is finished, he said.

Plastics suppliers say they may be able to use the ash produced in pyrolysis as well, particularly if the feedstock is uncontaminated scrap from the production process. Since some of the composites used in auto body panels consist of 50 percent inert filler, clean ash might be substituted for the limestone used now. But it is less likely that ash from shredder residue contaminated with other substances could be used.

Industry officials have been quick to label pyrolysis a form of recycling, but some environmentalists say it is similar to incineration, because the material is destroyed and some energy is used. "We do not consider incineration as recycling on this side of the environmental fence, and a lot of people put pyrolysis in the same category," said Lisa Collaton, a solid-waste specialist at the Environmental Action Foundation in Washington.

Added John Ruston of the Environmental Defense Fund in New York, "Pyrolysis is not recycling; it is pyrolysis."

Mr. Poston said G.M. and some plastic suppliers had run pyrolysis tests on shredder residue at two operations for processing old tires. He said that once the material reached operating temperature, it gave off enough gas to be self-sustaining without external fuel. The recovered oil is available for sale.

He said the company and its suppliers planned larger-scale tests to see if the approach was technically and economically feasible in commercial quantities. "We have done 5,000 pounds; now we are going to do a run of 50,000 pounds so we can see the true economics," Mr. Poston said.

MORE PLASTIC IN CARS

A group of plastic parts suppliers predicts that the amount of thermoset materials going into cars will almost double by 1995, to 423 million pounds, from 242 million pounds in 1990. That is in addition to thermoplastic materials, which can be melted and used again.

Officials involved in recycling say pyrolysis may have a place in materials disposal, after more valuable plastic parts of old cars and appliances have been pulled out for recycling. "Pyrolysis can be part of the waste-management approach, but we should not give up on recovering various plastic streams for re-use," said Michael Fisher, a technical director at the Council for Solid Waste Solutions, a plastics industry group.

Noting that it took metal recyclers several decades to refine techniques for separating different metals and alloys, he said that the plastics industry was just beginning the process. "There are 20 different types of plastic on an automobile," he said. "Some will be recycled, and some will go for pyrolysis."

Herschel Cutler, executive director of the Institute for Scrap Recycling Industries, said the institute was interested in pyrolysis, despite economic, technical and pollution problems with some other experiments. "There have been some plants in the past that were dismal failures," he said.

Nevertheless, he said, with the amount of plastic in cars rising, "we are still looking at it." He added, "We may see a new generation of pyrolytic activity that really can convert materials to oil, gas and carbon black."

CHAPTER 3

Environmental Crisis in the 21st Century

Widespread efforts toward reusing and recycling plastic could not forestall the environmental crisis that has already taken hold. "Of the roughly 8.3 billion metric tons of plastics produced worldwide since the 1950s, about 6.3 billion have been thrown away," Mike Ives notes in his 2018 article, "Whale's Death in Thailand Points to Global Scourge: Plastic in Oceans." As humanity has relied on plastic for its many innovations and conveniences, the Earth has paid the price. This chapter covers the impact the plastics industry has had in saturating landfills, clogging the oceans and contributing to climate change.

Plastic Surge

COLUMN | BY LYNN YAEGER | AUG. 26, 2007

MY CARBON FOOTPRINT is as tiny and delicate as Cinderella's. I don't drive a car (who needs one in Manhattan?), I barely know what a dishwasher is (who eats at home?), and believe it or not, I don't even have an air conditioner (it would ruin my Art Deco apartment).

So I would hardly describe myself as an environmentally tone-deaf hog who doesn't give a hoot about the planet, even as I waver deliciously between a Fendi handbag decorated with the picture of a horse and a Lanvin one imprinted with lurid cabbage roses — both of which, despite their four-figure price tags, are made of glistening plastic. (I have already rejected a clear Prada tote because, according to an indiscreet sales clerk, it melts after prolonged exposure to sunlight.)

It's neither the price nor the fact that these shiny new purses are made of a material once reserved for 14th Street that has me in a state of apoplexy. No, the problem is one of personal responsibility. Do I really want to be culpable for the deaths of millions of birds, fish and, in the end, the planet itself?

This deeply unfashion-friendly revelation came to me as I perused Alan Weisman's harrowing new book "The World Without Us" (St. Martin's Press), an environmental exposé that tells you in no uncertain terms what havoc your nylon Prada carryall will wreak a couple of seasons from now when you're sick of the sight of it.

You'll blithely send it to one of those thrift shops on the Upper East Side or sell it on eBay (unless it's sufficiently trashed, in which case it will head straight to the Salvation Army). But unlike your woven Bottega Veneta or burnished Mulberry bags, that homely nylon sack will spend its fashion afterlife choking animals to death or littering the beaches of Bora Bora for the next million or so years.

It isn't as if fashion types don't care about the earth. In fact, the holiday windows at Barneys New York will work a Rudolph the Recycling Reindeer theme this year; the clothing company Edun, along with many other progressive labels, proffers T-shirts made of organic cotton; and racks across the country are groaning with hemp purses and sweaters of woven bamboo. The problem is, I don't want a pullover made from a tree. I want a Marni duster rendered in faintly gleaming nylon and a pair of Marc Jacobs mouse flats molded from a clear substance reminiscent of Life Savers.

But Weisman's words ring in my ears: Think that Lanvin purse will languish as landfill? Think again. Plastics can break down into deathly, indigestible polymer particles, or wind up where they were never intended. Weisman's examples sent me right over the edge — sea otters choking on polyethylene six-pack rings; a sea turtle found dead with a comb, a length of nylon rope and the wheel of a toy truck, all jammed in its gut.

These anecdotes are so upsetting that I put my Lanvin-versus-Fendi dilemma on the back burner and ring up my friend Mickey Boardman, the deputy editorial director of Paper magazine and a sweetly militant vegetarian who refers to his designer wardrobe as cruelty-free. Hey, Mickey, I bet you never realized that your nasty plastic shoes are killing those little animals you profess to care so much about?

"It has semi-occurred to me that we're destroying the earth, and I do try to take a stand," says Mickey, who has taken to bringing his 10 Corso Como canvas shopping bag to the supermarket whenever he runs out of diet ginger ale. But even his newfound concern for the environment and my rising anxiety do not prevent him from purchasing a vinyl-wrapped Pucci tote shortly after we speak.

Maybe when he's ready to toss it, he should pitch it in the direction of Yeohlee Teng, the queen of quirky, environmentally conscious fabric. Her approach to design under her label, Yeohlee, is often post-apocalyptic. For a class project at Otis College of Art and Design, where she was a guest lecturer, Teng instructed students to imagine that the world as we know it is gone, and to design fabric using found materials: yarn, plastic bottles, etc. — kind of "Mad MaxMara."

Teng's conscience appears to be as clear as the see-through plastic raincoat she made in the early '90s, "large and comfortable, with the body's silhouette visible underneath," she recalls. It sounds madly chic. But will it be bobbing fatefully in the Pacific, to be joined all too soon by my brand-new Fendi?

I'm too ashamed to say.

Plastic Panic

BY LAUREN KERN | MARCH 9, 2011

IF YOU'VE BEEN FEELING safe and self-satisfied because you only buy BPA-free plastic, prepare to be freaked out (again). NPR reports on a study in Environmental Health Perspectives that found that more than 95 percent of 450 plastic items tested — ranging from baby bottles to deli packaging — released estrogenic chemicals when exposed to real-world stresses like microwaving or dishwashing or even sunlight.

"Sometimes the BPA-free products had even more activity than products known to contain BPA," Jon Hamilton writes. Hamilton is careful to point out that the health effects of such exposure are unclear (and that one of the study's authors has a financial interest in a company that makes nonestrogenic plastics), but the commenters aren't taking any chances. One reader, whose 4-year-old son was given a diagnosis of idiopathic breast bud development, wrote, "I am definitely throwing out all the plastic plates and cups we have been using."

The 'Great Pacific Garbage Patch' Is Ballooning, 87,000 Tons of Plastic and Counting

BY LIVIA ALBECK-RIPKA | MARCH 22, 2018

IN THE PACIFIC OCEAN between California and Hawaii, hundreds of miles from any major city, plastic bottles, children's toys, broken electronics, abandoned fishing nets and millions more fragments of debris are floating in the water — at least 87,000 tons' worth, researchers said Thursday.

In recent years, this notorious mess has become known as the Great Pacific Garbage Patch, a swirling oceanic graveyard where everyday objects get deposited by the currents. The plastics eventually disintegrate into tiny particles that often get eaten by fish and may ultimately enter our food chain.

A study published Thursday in the journal Scientific Reports quantified the full extent of the so-called garbage patch: It is four to 16 times bigger than previously thought, occupying an area roughly four times the size of California and comprising an estimated 1.8 trillion pieces of rubbish. While the patch was once thought to be more akin to a soup of nearly invisible microplastics, scientists now think most of the trash consists of larger pieces. And, they say, it is growing "exponentially."

"It's just quite alarming, because you are so far from the mainland," said Laurent Lebreton, the lead author of the study and an oceanographer with the Ocean Cleanup Foundation, a nonprofit that is developing systems to remove ocean trash and which funded the study. "There's no one around and you still see those common objects, like crates and bottles."

JUST ONE WORD: PLASTICS

In the late summer of 2015, Mr. Lebreton and his colleagues measured the amount of plastic debris in the patch by trawling it with nets and

A sample jar of plastic debris recovered from the Great Pacific Garbage Patch.

flying overhead to take aerial photographs. Though they also found glass, rubber and wood, 99.9 percent of what the researchers pulled out of the ocean was plastic.

They also recovered a startling number of abandoned plastic fishing nets, Mr. Lebreton said. These "ghost nets" made up almost half of the total weight of the debris. (One explanation is the patch's proximity to fishing grounds; another is that fishing material is designed to be resilient at sea and stays intact longer than other objects.)

"We found a few unexpected objects," Mr. Lebreton said. "Among them were plastic toys, which I found really sad, as some of them may have come from the tsunami in Japan," he added, referring to the 2011 disaster that sent millions of tons of debris into the ocean.

The researchers also fished out a '90s-era Game Boy cover, construction-site helmets and a toilet seat, as well as a number of objects with Japanese and Chinese inscriptions. Other objects, Mr. Lebreton said, had "little bite marks from fish."

Some sea turtles caught near the patch were eating so much plastic that it made up around three-quarters of their diet, according to the foundation.

THE GARBAGE PATCH IS NOT EXACTLY A 'PATCH'

After its discovery in the late '90s, the Great Pacific Garbage Patch took on an image in the popular imagination akin to an island or even a seventh continent made of trash. That myth was debunked, and the patch became understood as more like a region that looked like the rest of the ocean to the naked eye, but was polluted with tiny microplastics.

However the new study says that the microplastics, while still a problem, account for just 8 percent of the mass of the patch. Until now, most of the sampling used an ocean trawl designed to pick up small particles, and therefore, Mr. Lebreton said, underestimated the number of larger pieces of debris floating in the sea, like bottles, buoys and fishing nets.

"Most of the mass is actually large debris, ready to decompose into microplastic," Mr. Lebreton said.

Still, "it's not an island," Mr. Lebreton said. "It's very scattered." (A visual model, however, shows how the debris is condensed in one area in the ocean.)

"I think the name 'patch' is a little bit confusing," said Nancy Wallace, the director of the National Oceanic and Atmospheric Administration's Marine Debris Program, who was not involved in the study. Describing it that way, she said, gave the wrong impression that it "would be easy to go pick it up."

THERE MAY STILL BE TIME TO ACT

The worry is that, within a few decades, the larger pieces of debris could break up into microplastics, which are much harder to remove from the ocean. "It's like a ticking time bomb," said Joost Dubois, a spokesman for the Ocean Cleanup Foundation.

The foundation says it would be almost impossible to remove the plastic already in the patch by traditional methods, like nets attached to boats. Instead, the group has developed a mechanical system that floats through the water and concentrates the plastics into denser areas that can then be collected by boats and taken back to shore to be recycled.

The foundation plans to launch the first such system this summer from Alameda, Calif.

LIVIA ALBECK-RIPKA is a freelance journalist based in New York and Melbourne, Australia.

Whale's Death in Thailand Points to Global Scourge: Plastic in Oceans

BY MIKE IVES | JUNE 4, 2018

HONG KONG — Hundreds of turtles, dolphins and whales become stranded every year on Thailand's beaches after plastic impedes their mobility or clogs their insides. Some are lifeless on arrival, biologists say, and their deaths barely register with the public.

But the survival of a pilot whale that washed ashore in southern Thailand last week, in critical condition and with a belly full of black plastic bags, became a cause célèbre for ordinary people. And its death a few days later was a vivid reminder of a staggering global problem: plastics in the oceans and seas.

"Many in the region and around the world are extremely concerned about such incidents," Suresh Valiyaveettil, a chemist at the National University of Singapore who studies how polymers interact with living systems, said in an email. "Considering the amount of plastic in the ocean, unfortunately, such incidents are going to be more common in the near future."

After the whale's death on Friday, a necropsy showed that it had washed ashore in the southern province of Songkhla with nearly 18 pounds of plastic in its stomach. Veterinarians had tried to save its life all week, to no avail.

Some in Thailand went on social media over the weekend to express their anguish and outrage.

"I feel so sorry for this poor thing," one user, Nichapa Samranrat, wrote on Facebook. "I wouldn't even dare to throw out a small piece of rubbish. Why are some people so lacking in common sense?"

The whale also drew sympathy from around the world.

Of the roughly 8.3 billion metric tons of plastics produced worldwide since the 1950s, about 6.3 billion have been thrown away, according to a 2017 study in the journal Science Advances. The study said that if current production and waste-management trends continued, about 12 billion metric tons of plastic waste would be in landfills or the natural environment by 2050.

A need for packaging is the main driver of plastics consumption globally, and the study's authors said that packaging made up 54 percent of the nonfiber plastic thrown away in 2015.

A separate study that year in the journal Science found that the six countries producing the most "mismanaged plastic waste" in 2010 were in the Asia-Pacific region. China topped the list, followed by Indonesia, the Philippines, Vietnam, Sri Lanka and Thailand.

The study also said that an estimated eight million metric tons of plastic waste made its way into the world's oceans each year — equivalent to "five plastic grocery bags filled with plastic for every foot of coastline in the world," the study's lead author, Jenna Jambeck, told The New York Times.

Water pollution has been making headlines across Southeast Asia in recent months. First the Indonesian island of Bali declared a "garbage emergency" late last year after garbage washed up on its beaches. And in April, President Rodrigo Duterte of the Philippines ordered the closing of a popular resort island, saying that the water around it posed a danger to public health.

In Thailand, more than 300 endangered sea turtles and between 100 and 150 dolphins and whales are stranded on local beaches every year after ingesting plastic or being somehow caught up in it, said Thon Thamrongnawasawat, a fisheries expert at Kasetsart University in Bangkok, citing government figures.

Last week, the European Union proposed banning several single-use plastic products in an attempt to reduce an estimated $250 billion or more of marine pollution over the next dozen years. Dr. Thon said he was urging the Thai government to do the same.

"We don't want to be the country that everyone blames in the future if we do nothing," he said.

Dr. Thon added that in the short term, he was working with the government on a plan for a consumer tax on plastic shopping bags.

But Anchalee Pipattanawattanakul, an activist with Greenpeace in Thailand, said the advocacy group was calling instead for a tax on companies that produced plastic bags, as well as more transparency from the Thai government on how much plastic waste was actually being generated.

"We need more pressure on the producer," she said.

RYN JIRENUWAT contributed reporting from Bangkok.

Before You Flush Your Contact Lenses, You Might Want to Know This

BY VERONIQUE GREENWOOD | AUG. 19, 2018

Flushing disposable contacts down the toilet or washing them down the drain may contribute to the problem of microplastic pollution, researchers said.

IF YOU THROW OUT your contact lenses every day or so, you're not alone — more than 45 million people in the United States wear contacts, and many of them use disposable versions of the little plastic hemispheres.

But if they are not tossed out correctly, contact lenses may have a dark side.

Research presented Sunday at the American Chemical Society's meeting in Boston showed that 20 percent of more than 400 contact wearers who were randomly recruited in an online survey flushed used contacts down the toilet or washed them down the sink, rather than putting them in the garbage.

When the lenses make their way to a wastewater treatment facility, they do not biodegrade easily, the researchers report, and they may fragment and make their way into surface water. There, they can cause environmental damage and may add to the growing problem of microplastic pollution. A 2015 study found that there were 93,000 to 236,000 metric tons of microplastic swirling in the ocean.

Filters keep some nonbiological waste out of wastewater treatment plants, said Rolf Halden, the director of the Center for Environmental Health Engineering at Arizona State University, and Charles Rolsky, a graduate student and the study's lead author. (Dr. Halden uses contact lenses; Mr. Rolsky wears glasses.) But contacts are so flexible that they can fold up and make their way through. The researchers interviewed workers at such facilities, who confirmed that they had spotted lenses in the waste.

Next, the team submerged contacts in chambers where bacteria are used to break down biological waste at a treatment plant. They found that even after seven days of exposure, the lenses appeared intact, though lab analysis detected small changes in the material.

"These are medical devices — you would not expect them to be super-biodegradable," Dr. Halden said. "Good for the contact lens wearer during use, not so good when the things get out into the environment."

Then, going through about nine pounds of treated waste, Mr. Rolsky and a colleague found two fragments of contact lens, implying that while microorganisms might not make much of a mark, physical processing might break them into pieces.

Tiny bits of plastic from many sources have been spotted in the oceans and other bodies of water, where they may be ingested by fish, corals and other animals. The fragments can carry high loads of pollutants absorbed from their surroundings, so the organisms get a dose of these substances as well.

After processing, treated waste is often spread on fields. If fragments of contacts are in the mixture, they or the substances they've picked up may be washed by rain into surface water, the researchers conjecture. They estimate that billions of contact lenses — weighing at least 22 metric tons — may be flushed in the United States every year.

Contact lens packages don't currently tell users how to dispose of them, said Dr. Halden, who suggested that companies should add labels recommending that contacts be put in the garbage rather than washed down the drain. He pointed out that some manufacturers have already begun recycling programs to reclaim the plastic from lenses. While contact lenses are far from the largest source of microplastic pollution in water, they appear to be a readily avoidable one.

Mr. Rolsky said the findings had given him an additional incentive to stick with his preference for wearing glasses. "This just gives me a reason," he said with a laugh, "to solidify that for the rest of time."

Just a Few Pieces of Plastic Can Kill Sea Turtles

BY KAREN WEINTRAUB | SEPT. 13, 2018

A new study shows that especially for young turtles, ingesting just a little more than a dozen pieces of plastic in the ocean can be lethal.

ALL OVER THE WORLD, sea turtles are swallowing bits of plastic floating in the ocean, mistaking them for tasty jellyfish, or just unable to avoid the debris that surrounds them.

Now, a new study out of Australia is trying to catalog the damage.

While some sea turtles have been found to have swallowed hundreds of bits of plastic, just 14 pieces significantly increases their risk of death, according to the study, published Thursday in Scientific Reports.

Young sea turtles are most vulnerable, the study found, because they drift with currents where the floating debris also accumulate, and because they are less choosy than adults about what they will eat.

Worldwide, more than half of all sea turtles from all seven species have eaten plastic debris, estimated Britta Denise Hardesty, the paper's senior author and a principal research scientist with the Commonwealth Scientific and Industrial Research Organization in Tasmania. "It doesn't matter where you are, you will find plastic," she said.

Six of the seven species of sea turtles are considered threatened, although many populations are recovering.

The study examined data from two sets of Australian sea turtles: necropsies of 246 animals and 706 records from a national strandings database. Both showed animals that died for reasons unrelated to eating plastic had less plastic in their guts than those that died of unknown causes or direct ingestion.

But the deaths are hard to pin down. "Just because a turtle has a plastic in it, you can't say that it died from it, except in very extenuating

Green sea turtles feed on a blue blubber jellyfish in Byron Bay, Australia. Green turtles have been known to ingest floating plastic because of its resemblance to jellyfish.

circumstances," Dr. Hardesty said. Even a single piece of plastic can occasionally cause death. In one case a turtle was found with its digestive tract blocked by a soft piece of plastic; in another, its intestine was perforated by a sharp piece of plastic.

In others, a variety of plastic material was found inside their digestive tracts — as many as 329 pieces in one sea turtle. Because of their anatomy, sea turtles cannot vomit up something once they've swallowed it, Dr. Hardesty said, meaning it either passes through their gut or gets stuck.

For a juvenile of typical size, half the animals would be expected to die if they ingested 17 plastic items, the study concluded. Sea turtles can live to be 80 or more years old, Dr. Hardesty said, with juveniles too young to reproduce ranging up to age 20 to 30.

The study's innovation was to try to determine this inflection point, where the load of plastic becomes lethal, said T. Todd Jones, a supervisory research biologist with the National Oceanic and Atmospheric Administration in Hawaii.

"There's always been this question of when is plastic too much?" Dr. Jones said.

An animal that swallows a lot of plastic might appear healthy, Dr. Jones said, but might be weakened by plastic in its gut limiting food absorption.

Mark Hamann, a turtle expert and associate professor at James Cook University in Townsville, Australia, said he hoped that studies like this one would provide a sense of the scope of the problem. In some areas with high levels of plastic pollution, like the Mediterranean and the southern Atlantic Ocean, turtles are unable to avoid the debris, while in other areas it is less of a problem.

"We know individual turtles are dying, but we don't know yet whether enough turtles are dying to cause population decline, and that's where we're heading to now," Dr. Hamann said.

Jennifer Lynch, a research biologist with the National Institute of Standards and Technology in Hawaii, took issue with the way the study measured vulnerability to plastic.

In her own research, she has seen animals that aren't harmed after swallowing 300 pieces of plastic, so she doesn't believe that 14 pieces pose such a high risk of death. "They ate a lot of plastic but it did them no harm," Dr. Lynch said of the animals she's examined. "They swallow it and they poop it out."

The difference between the two studies, Dr. Lynch said, was the health of the animals. "There's a very strong bias in their study toward very sick, dead animals," she said. "We looked only at live, healthy animals that died because they drowned on a fishhook."

Dr. Lynch said the new study should have focused on the weight of the plastic rather than the number of pieces. A single piece could range from a speck of microplastic to an entire snack bag, she noted.

"It's just that this magic number of 14 pieces I think is too low," Dr. Lynch said. "I think we have a lot more to do before we know what concentration of plastic causes physiological and anatomical impacts."

Dr. Lynch does agree that sea turtles are eating too much plastic. "We have to get this pollutant under control if we don't want to kill half of our sea turtles."

The vast majority of plastic off Hawaii, she said, comes from the international fishing industry, which is prohibited from dumping its old fishing lines and crates overboard, but often does it anyway — and faces no consequences. "Teeth is what's needed," Dr. Lynch said.

Dr. Hardesty said she thinks it's possible to reduce the turtles' exposure to plastic with a variety of approaches, from incentives to bans for high-impact, frequently littered items.

"The stuff that ends up in the ocean was in somebody's hand at some point in time," she said.

Microplastics Find Their Way Into Your Gut, a Pilot Study Finds

BY DOUGLAS QUENQUA | OCT. 22, 2018

Researchers looked for microplastics in stool samples of people from eight countries. "The results were astonishing," they said.

IN THE NEXT 60 seconds, people around the world will purchase one million plastic bottles and two million plastic bags. By the end of the year, we will produce enough bubble wrap to encircle the Equator 10 times.

Though it will take more than 1,000 years for most of these items to degrade, many will soon break apart into tiny shards known as microplastics, trillions of which have been showing up in the oceans, fish, tap water and even table salt.

Now, we can add one more microplastic repository to the list: the human gut.

In a pilot study with a small sample size, researchers looked for microplastics in stool samples of eight people from Finland, Italy, Japan, the Netherlands, Poland, Russia, the United Kingdom and Austria. To their surprise, every single sample tested positive for the presence of a variety of microplastics.

"This is the first study of its kind, so we did a pilot trial to see if there are any microplastics detectable at all," said Philipp Schwabl, a gastroenterologist at the Medical University of Vienna and lead author of the study. "The results were astonishing."

There are no certain health implications for their findings, and they hope to complete a broader study with the methods they have developed.

Microplastics — defined as pieces less than 0.2 inches long, roughly the size of a grain of rice — have become a major concern for environmental researchers over the past decade. Several studies have found high levels of microplastics in marine life, and last year, microplastics were detected in 83 percent of tap water samples around the world (the highest contamination rate belonged to the United States, where 94 percent of samples were contaminated).

Most microplastics are the unintended result of larger plastics breaking apart, and the United States, Canada and other countries have banned the use of tiny plastic beads in beauty products.

Researchers have long suspected microplastics would eventually be found in the human gut. One study estimated that people who regularly eat shellfish may be consuming as much as 11,000 plastic pieces per year.

The new paper, which was presented Monday at a gastroenterology conference in Vienna, could provide support for marine biologists who have long warned of the dangers posed by microplastics in our oceans. But the paper suggests that microplastics are entering our bodies through other means, as well.

"The fact that so many different polymers were measured suggests a wide range of contamination sources," said Stephanie Wright, an environmental health scientist at Kings College London who was not involved in the study. Two of the eight participants also said they did not consume seafood.

To conduct the study, they selected volunteers from each country who kept food diaries for a week and provided stool samples. Dr. Schwabl and his colleagues analyzed the samples with a spectrometer.

Up to nine different kinds of plastics were detected, ranging in size from .002 to .02 inches. The most common plastics detected were polypropylene and polyethylene terephthalate — both major components of plastic bottles and caps.

Still, Dr. Schwabl cautioned against jumping to conclusions about the origins of the plastic.

"Most participants drank liquids from plastic bottles, but also fish and seafood ingestion was common," he said. "It is highly likely that food is being contaminated with plastics during various steps of food processing or as a result of packaging."

Whether microplastics pose a health risk to humans is largely unknown, though they have been found to cause some damage in fish and other animals. Additionally, the microplastics detected in the current study are too large to be a serious threat, Dr. Wright said.

"But what may be of greater concern for these large microplastics is whether any associated chemical contaminants leach off during gut passage and accumulate in tissues," she said.

The concentration of contaminants — 20 microplastic particles per 10 grams of stool — was relatively low, she said.

Nonetheless, Dr. Schwabl said the results were more than enough to investigate further.

"Now that we know there is microplastic present in stool, and we know how to detect it, we aim to perform a larger study including more participants," he said.

European Parliament Approves Ban on Single-Use Plastics

BY CEYLAN YEGINSU | OCT. 25, 2018

LONDON — The European Parliament has overwhelmingly approved a ban on single-use plastics such as straws, plates, cutlery and cotton-swab sticks in Europe by 2021, joining a global shift as environmentalists emphasize the urgency of halting the use of materials that are detrimental to the planet.

Under the proposal, approved on a vote of 571 to 53 on Wednesday, 10 single-use plastics that most often end up in the ocean will be prohibited in the European Union, as well as oxo-degradable plastics, such as bags or fast-food container packaging.

The use of other plastics such as single-use burger and sandwich boxes that don't have practical alternatives at this point will be reduced by at least 25 percent by 2025, and 90 percent of beverage bottles will be recycled, under the proposal.

The European Parliament will next enter into negotiations with the European Council of government ministers for the 28 member states, who are expected to make a final decision on the legislation by Dec. 16.

"We have adopted the most ambitious legislation against single-use plastics," said Frédérique Ries, the member of the European Parliament who drafted the bill.

"Today's vote paves the way to a forthcoming and ambitious directive," she added. "It is essential in order to protect the marine environment and reduce the costs of environmental damage attributed to plastic pollution in Europe, estimated at 22 billion euros by 2030."

The European Commission put forward the legislation in May, after its research found that plastics made up 80 percent of marine litter on European beaches, posing a major threat to coastal biodiversity. The commission found that marine litter costs the European Union $295 million to $793 million per year.

The World Economic Forum estimates that 90 percent of the plastic ending up in the oceans comes from 10 major rivers, and that currently there are 50 million tons of plastic in the world's oceans that could take centuries to degrade. This year the forum warned that there would be more plastic than fish in weight in oceans by 2050.

In February, Marine scientists in Ireland released a study that showed they had found plastic in 73 percent of 233 deep-sea fish from the Northwest Atlantic Ocean — one of the highest reported frequencies of microplastic occurrence in fish worldwide, according to experts from the National University of Ireland.

A small pilot study presented this month said that researchers had found a variety of microplastics in stool samples of eight people from Austria, Finland, Italy, Japan, the Netherlands, Poland, Russia and the United Kingdom — which Philipp Schwabl, a gastroenterologist at the Medical University of Vienna and lead author of the study, called "astonishing."

The European Federation of Waste Management and Environmental Services, or FEAD, the body representing waste-management companies in Europe, welcomed the Parliament's vote but highlighted the need for fully recyclable packaging items.

"I am confident that E.U. negotiators will succeed in deciding by December 2018 on a level of mandatory recycled content, to be transposed into E.U. law by 2025, which will trigger the uptake of plastic recyclates in beverage bottles," Jean-Marc Boursier, the president of FEAD, said, referring to raw materials processed at waste plants.

"By doing so, the E.U. will finally experience a circular shift that is long overdue," Mr. Boursier said.

In Britain, the push to reduce the use of plastics has accelerated, with McDonalds announcing in June that it would phase out plastic straws in its 1,361 restaurants in Britain, the Church of England encouraging the change and the government planning to legislate against the use of the straws.

Ocean Cleanup Plastic Collector Heading Home. In Pieces.

BY ERIC NAGOURNEY | JAN. 3, 2019

IT SET SAIL from San Francisco Bay in September amid high hopes and more than a little fanfare, its destination the Great Pacific Garbage Patch.

The goal was for the giant floating boom to make a dent in the vast archipelago of plastic that is choking the seas between California and Hawaii.

But this week, the nonprofit group that developed the boom said it would be towed back to port — in two pieces.

"We are, of course, quite bummed about this," the Dutch organization, the Ocean Cleanup, wrote on a blog chronicling the device's triumphs and travails.

By some estimates, the Great Pacific Garbage Patch consists of more than 80,000 tons of waste and debris, tossed together by the currents into a sort of island of lost toys, minus the island. As it grows, scientists say, so does the danger it poses to the health of the ocean.

The 2,000-foot-long boom, which arrived at the garbage patch after a voyage of about 1,400 miles, was designed to trap the trash so that it could be returned to shore. The Ocean Cleanup's goals were ambitious: 150,000 pounds of plastic in Year 1, with more booms to follow. Within five years, the group hoped, half the debris would be collected.

But on Monday, the organization said that in a routine inspection over the weekend, it found that an end-section of the boom almost 60 feet long — 18 meters — had detached. The boom will be taken back to shore as soon as weather allows, the group said.

The Ocean Cleanup said it appeared that material fatigue and "local stress concentration" might have caused the fracture in the multimillion-dollar structure.

The Ocean Cleanup launched its first cleanup system from San Francisco to the ocean last year. The group that created it said material fatigue and "local stress concentration" might have caused a fracture in the multimillion-dollar structure.

Skeptics had raised doubts about whether the boom, known as Wilson, would do much good and whether it could hold up to the forces of nature.

"It is very difficult to predict what will take place in these very dynamic ocean environments," Nicholas Mallos, director of the Trash Free Seas program at the Ocean Conservancy, said Thursday.

Mr. Mallos praised the Ocean Cleanup for helping turn world attention to a major environmental problem. But he said stopping plastics before they enter the ocean from beaches and local waterways was a more effective approach, along with reducing overall plastic use.

The inventor behind the boom, Boyan Slat, had himself warned of possible setbacks. "First of all," he said before the boom was sent out, "it's something that we haven't really been able to test very well."

And, in fact, in the early weeks of its deployment, the device, which has no crew and is powered by the sun, had trouble retaining the debris it collected. Its return to port, the Ocean Cleanup said, offers a chance to address that.

"Although we would have liked to end the year on a more positive note," the group said, "we believe these teething troubles are solvable, and the cleanup of the Great Pacific Garbage Patch will be operational in 2019."

Whale Is Found Dead in Italy With 48 Pounds of Plastic in Its Stomach

BY ILIANA MAGRA | APRIL 2, 2019

MORE THAN 48 POUNDS of plastic, including disposable dishes, a corrugated tube, shopping bags and a detergent package with its bar code still visible, were found inside a dead sperm whale in Italy, the World Wildlife Fund said on Monday.

The whale, a young female, washed ashore in Porto Cervo, a seaside resort in the north of the Italian island of Sardinia. It was also carrying a fetus "in an advanced state of decomposition," the fund said.

This was the latest in a grim international collection of whale carcasses burdened by dozens of pounds of plastic trash.

Last month, a whale was found dead on a Philippine beach with 88 pounds of plastic in its body. More than 1,000 assorted pieces of plastic were discovered inside a decomposing whale in Indonesia in November. A sperm whale died in Spain last year after being unable to digest more than 60 pounds of plastic trash.

"Plastic is one of the worst enemies of marine species," the World Wildlife Fund said on Monday.

The whale in Porto Cervo was found on Thursday, according to a Facebook post by SeaMe Sardinia, a nonprofit organization that studies marine mammals. The cause of death is still being investigated, but the quantity of plastic found is unusual for a whale of its size, about 26 feet, the World Wildlife Fund said.

"The amount of plastic found in the cetacean's digestive tract was practically intact, and the proportion between the size of the animal and the ingested plastic is particularly significant," it said in a statement on Monday.

Europe is the second-largest producer of plastics in the world, "dumping 150,000-500,000 tons of macroplastics and 70,000-130,000 tons of microplastics in the sea every year," according to a report the fund published in June.

Surveys suggest that has left the Mediterranean with some of the highest microplastic pollution levels in the world.

Partly in response to such findings, the European Union Parliament voted last week to approve a ban on many single-use plastic products, including disposable plastic straws, cutlery and plates.

Those measures are scheduled to take effect by 2021. On Sunday, in a Facebook post that featured a picture of the dead whale, Italy's environment minister, Sergio Costa, promised his country would be one of the first to carry out the ban.

This sort of pollution, he wrote, "afflicts the whole marine world, not just Italy, of course, but every country in the world has the duty to apply the policies to fight it: not today, yesterday."

"Is there still someone who says that these are not important problems?" he asked.

Ocean-Clogging Microplastics Also Pollute the Air, Study Finds

BY LIAM STACK | APRIL 18, 2019

RESEARCHERS IN FRANCE said this week that they found thousands and thousands of microplastic particles raining down on a secluded spot in the Pyrenees, 75 miles from the nearest city.

Their study, published in the journal Nature Geoscience, suggests that microplastics — long known as a source of water pollution — may also travel by air, spreading their ill effects far from dense population centers.

Deonie Allen, one of the lead researchers, said the five-month study was "the first step toward looking at microplastics as an airborne pollutant." Steve Allen, another researcher, called their findings "scary."

"We kind of expected to find plastics there, but we certainly were not prepared for the numbers we found," Mr. Allen said in an interview. "It was astounding: 11,400 pieces of microplastic per square meter per month, on average."

WHAT ARE MICROPLASTICS?

Microplastics are pieces of plastic debris that measure less than five millimeters long, roughly the size of a sesame seed, according to the National Oceanic and Atmospheric Administration.

But they can also be much smaller than five millimeters. The fragments found by the Pyrenees study were generally 10 to 300 microns across, with most clocking in at roughly 50 microns, Dr. Allen said. For comparison, a human hair is about 70 microns wide.

"These are invisible atmospheric pollutants," she said.

Microplastics can come from a variety of sources, including everyday items like plastic bottles or disposable contact lenses that break down into smaller pieces over time. According to Dr. Allen, a lot of microplastic pollution comes from cities, landfills and farms that are sprayed with "wastewater treatment sludge, which is loaded with microplastics."

Microbeads, which are found in some hygiene products like toothpaste, are another source of microplastic pollution. Concern over their environmental impact has led some governments, including Britain's, to ban the manufacture of products that contain them.

WHERE ARE THEY FOUND?

They may be everywhere. Or, at least, wherever the water and wind can take them.

In the ocean, microplastics contribute to phenomena like the Great Pacific Garbage Patch, a swirling gyre of more than 87,000 tons of trash that lies hundreds of miles from shore.

But the Pyrenees study, a collaboration between the University of Strathclyde in Scotland and the French National Center for Scientific Research at the University of Toulouse, suggests they may also be a source of pollution in the air and on land.

"At this point there is a lot of knowledge about oceans as a driver of microplastic pollution, which is creating some backlash against plastics," Mr. Allen said. "But we are still learning that we can't get away from it because it is also in the air."

The study took place in a remote spot four miles from the nearest village and roughly 75 miles from the nearest city, Toulouse. Researchers, taking samples from two separate monitoring devices, found that 365 pieces of microplastic per square meter rained down from the sky each day.

Mr. Allen compared airborne microplastics to dust from the Sahara, which has long been known to travel by wind across the ocean to the United States and the Caribbean.

"At 450 microns, it can still travel 3,500 kilometers," he said. "Plastics are not as dense, they are about half the weight and they are irregularly shaped, so aerodynamically, it is easier for the particles to be lifted into the air."

HOW MUCH DAMAGE CAN THEY DO?

Microplastics have been found to harm animals, including insects and marine species, in a number of ways, but more research needs to be done to determine their effect on humans, researchers said.

Mr. Allen said microplastics had been shown to "block up the gut" in fish and insects.

"The chemicals that make up the plastic, we know they have an impact on the animal endocrine system and the lymphatic system," which regulate the production of hormones and the elimination of bodily toxins, he said.

In an example of plastic's gut-blocking effects on a larger scale, a dead sperm whale washed ashore this month on the Italian island of Sardinia with 48 pounds of plastic in its stomach, including microplastics as well as larger items like a corrugated plastic tube and shopping bags.

Dr. Allen said microplastic could also change the chemical composition of the environment in small but significant ways, for example, by absorbing pheromones that fish and insects depend on to trigger their fight-or-flight response.

"When you put plastic into that environment, it absorbs that chemical, which means those protection or defense responses are no longer occurring," she said. "It is not just about biological impacts inside the animal; it also impacts the environment it is living in."

Researchers are increasingly confident about the ubiquity of microplastics in human life.

A study published in 2017 found microplastics in 83 percent of tap water samples collected from around the world, including 94 percent of samples from the United States, which had the highest rate of contamination.

A study published last year found a variety of microplastics in stool samples from eight people from Finland, Italy, Japan, the Netherlands, Poland, Russia, Britain and Austria. Another study estimated that people who frequently eat shellfish could ingest as many as 11,000 pieces of microplastic every year.

Food Delivery Apps Are Drowning China in Plastic

BY RAYMOND ZHONG AND CAROLYN ZHANG | **MAY 28, 2019**

The noodles and barbecue arrive within 30 minutes. The containers they come in could be around for hundreds of years thereafter.

BEIJING — In all likelihood, the enduring physical legacy of China's internet boom will not be the glass-and-steel office complexes or the fancy apartments for tech elites.

It will be the plastic.

The astronomical growth of food delivery apps in China is flooding the country with takeout containers, utensils and bags. And the country's patchy recycling system isn't keeping up. The vast majority of this plastic ends up discarded, buried or burned with the rest of the trash, researchers and recyclers say.

Scientists estimate that the online takeout business in China was responsible for 1.6 million tons of packaging waste in 2017, a ninefold jump from two years before. That includes 1.2 million tons of plastic containers, 175,000 tons of disposable chopsticks, 164,000 tons of plastic bags and 44,000 tons of plastic spoons.

Put together, it is more than the amount of residential and commercial trash of all kinds disposed of each year by the city of Philadelphia. The total for 2018 grew to an estimated two million tons.

People in China still generate less plastic waste, per capita, than Americans. But researchers estimate that nearly three-quarters of China's plastic waste ends up in inadequately managed landfills or out in the open, where it can easily make its way into the sea. More plastic enters the world's oceans from China than from any other country. Plastic can take centuries to break down undersea.

Recyclers manage to return some of China's plastic trash into usable form to feed the nation's factories. The country recycles around a quarter of its plastic, government statistics show, compared with less than 10 percent in the United States.

But in China, takeout boxes do not end up recycled, by and large. They must be washed first. They weigh so little that scavengers must gather a huge number to amass enough to sell to recyclers.

"Half a day's work for just a few pennies. It isn't worth it," said Ren Yong, 40, a garbage collector at a downtown Shanghai office building. He said he threw takeout containers out.

For many overworked or merely lazy people in urban China, the leading takeout platforms Meituan and Ele.me are replacing cooking or eating out as the preferred means of obtaining nourishment. Delivery is so cheap, and the apps offer such generous discounts, that it is now possible to believe that ordering a single cup of coffee for delivery is a sane, reasonable thing to do.

Yuan Ruqian knows that it is not. Yet she, too, has succumbed.

Like the time she was craving ice cream, but a newly opened Dippin' Dots store seemed so far away. Or when she orders delivery for lunch, which is nearly every day.

Asked about the trash she generates, Ms. Yuan, 27, who works in finance in Shanghai, said: "Laziness is the root of all evil."

The transformation of daily life has been swift. Meituan says it delivered 6.4 billion food orders last year, a nearly 60 percent jump from 2017. Those orders were worth $42 billion in total, meaning the average order was $6.50 — about enough for a decent meal for one in a big Chinese city.

Ele.me — the name means "Are you hungry?" and is pronounced "UH-luh-muh" — has not disclosed similar figures. But across China's major takeout apps, orders worth a combined $70 billion were delivered in 2018, according to the analysis firm iResearch.

By comparison, online food delivery sales in the United States are expected to total $19 billion this year, according to Statista. Uber says its Uber Eats service generated $7.9 billion in orders worldwide last year. GrubHub reported $5.1 billion in food sales and 159 million orders in 2018, implying an average order value of $32.

At rush hour, deliverymen leave takeout orders in the lobbies of office buildings to save time.

Around the world, the convenience of such services comes with costs that can be easy to overlook. Labor controversies, for instance. Or roads made more hazardous by takeout couriers zooming around on motorbikes. Plastic waste is just as easily ignored, even when it is being generated and mismanaged on a titanic scale.

China is home to a quarter of all plastic waste that is dumped out in the open. Scientists estimate that the Yangtze River emptied 367,000 tons of plastic debris into the sea in 2015, more than any other river in the world, and twice the amount carried by the Ganges in India and Bangladesh. The world's third and fourth most polluting rivers are also in China.

Takeout apps may be indirectly encouraging restaurants to use more plastic. Restaurants in China that do business through Meituan and Ele.me say they are so dependent on customer ratings that they would rather use heavier containers, or sheathe an order in an extra layer of plastic wrap, than risk a bad review because of a spill.

"Meituan is deeply committed to reducing the environmental impact of food delivery," the company said in a statement, pointing to initiatives such as allowing users to choose not to receive disposable tableware.

The e-commerce titan Alibaba, which owns Ele.me, declined to comment.

This deluge of trash might not be such a big problem were China not in the middle of a monumental, if flawed, effort to fix its recycling system. Recycling has long been a gritty, unregulated affair in the country, one driven less by green virtue than by the business opportunity in extracting value out of other people's leavings.

The government now wants a recycling industry that doesn't spoil the environment or sicken workers. The transition hasn't been smooth.

China recently banned many types of scrap from being imported into the country, hoping that recyclers would focus on processing domestic material instead. That killed off a lucrative business for those recyclers, and left American cities scrambling to find new dumping grounds for their cardboard and plastic. Some cities have been forced to end their recycling programs.

Other policies may inadvertently be causing fewer recyclables to be collected from China's homes and offices. In Beijing, many scavengers who do this work have fallen victim to an aggressive government campaign to "improve the quality of the city's population," a euphemism for driving out migrant workers from the countryside.

To clean up the filthy air in Beijing, the government has also clamped down on "small, scattered polluting enterprises" in the capital region. Inspectors have since closed down hundreds of dingy backyard workshops that cleaned and processed plastic scrap.

Not everyone mourns the loss. For years, Mao Da, an environmental researcher, has studied the plastic industry in Wen'an County, near Beijing. Workers there used to sort through food and medical waste by hand, he said. Nonrecyclable material was buried in pits near farmland.

"It was an environmental and public health catastrophe," Mr. Mao said.

So far, though, the crackdown hasn't caused large, professionally managed recycling companies to fill the void. Instead, it has left the entire business in limbo.

"You've got fewer people collecting scrap, fewer people transporting it and fewer people processing it," said Chen Liwen, the founder of Zero-Waste Villages, a nonprofit that promotes recycling in rural China. "The overall recycling rate has definitely fallen."

In Chifeng, a small city northeast of Beijing, Zhang Jialin is pondering life after recycling.

For years, Mr. Zhang and his wife bought plastic scrap and ground it into chips. But the local authorities have stepped up environmental inspections. The city has slated Mr. Zhang's street for demolition. He and other recyclers believe it is because officials consider their scrap-yards an eyesore. The Chifeng government didn't respond to a request for comment.

"What I do is environmental protection," Mr. Zhang, 45, said. "I don't let stuff get thrown everywhere. I break it down. I wash it."

He continued: "So why do the environmental protection authorities target me as if I were harming environmental protection? That's what I don't get."

RAYMOND ZHONG is a technology reporter. Prior to joining The Times in 2017, he covered India's fast-moving economy from New Delhi for The Wall Street Journal.

Recyclers Cringe as Southeast Asia Says It's Sick of the West's Trash

BY MIKE IVES | JUNE 7, 2019

TELOK GONG, MALAYSIA — Black sedans with government plates raced through a town near Malaysia's main seaport, flashing blue sirens as they approached rogue trash dumps.

The raid, in the town of Telok Gong this week, was among the latest efforts by officials to shut down unlicensed dumps holding plastic scrap imported from the United States and other rich countries.

"Everybody knows those dumps are illegal," said Modh Faiz Tamsir, a butcher hawking fly-covered beef in a parking lot on Telok Gong's main drag. "We don't like them."

After China, once the world's primary dumping ground, abruptly imposed restrictions on "foreign garbage" in late 2017, countries across Southeast Asia began taking in the West's plastic waste.

Within months, Malaysia, which has a sizable ethnic Chinese population, had replaced China as the world's largest importer of plastic scrap. But this country, and others across the region, soon saw the waste as an environmental nightmare, and a heavy backlash has begun. With public support, some advocacy groups have urged officials to permanently ban the import of plastic waste.

But at a time when the world is awash in such plastic, some experts worry that this backlash could block the flow of raw material to Southeast Asia's aboveboard recyclers and manufacturers — and raise the chances that plastic scrap will end up in rivers, oceans, dumps and illegal burn sites.

By imposing blanket bans on imported waste, "you're potentially risking damaging the good recyclers' business," said Kakuko Nagatani-Yoshida, the United Nations Environment Program's coordinator on chemicals and waste in the Asia-Pacific region.

"When those people lose a business opportunity, then in the future you have fewer options for waste management," she added. "And I don't think any government should have fewer options; you always need more."

China's abrupt waste restrictions of 2017 were a response to years of pollution there by low-end recycling. They caused anxiety across a vast supply chain that includes waste companies and municipal recyclers in the United States and other developed economies.

"The exporter countries' pants were on fire," said Yuyun Ismawati, a co-founder of the Indonesian environmental group BaliFokus. "They realized they had underestimated China's seriousness."

Around the same time, unlicensed trash dumps, many of them owned by mainland Chinese investors, began appearing in the back alleys of Telok Gong and other towns near Southeast Asian ports.

"They just popped out of nowhere two years ago," said Soh Ah Boon, the Malaysian owner of a junkyard about 15 miles by car from Telok Gong that collects material from local sources.

By March 2018, the peak of the surge, Malaysia was importing about 139,000 tons of plastic waste per month, up from about 22,000 tons per month a year earlier, according to official trade data analyzed by Khor Yu Leng, an economist in Singapore who studies Southeast Asian commodities. The United States was the largest source, followed by Japan, Britain and Germany, she said.

As plastic imports rose across Southeast Asia, pollution became more noticeable — typically in the form of trash-clogged rivers or smoke from ragtag incineration sites, according to environmental groups.

Local opposition grew, too.

"Who would like it when someone comes to your neighborhood and tears the place up?" Mr. Soh said at his junkyard between drags of a cigarette.

In response, Southeast Asian governments issued waste-import restrictions of various shapes, sizes and durations. Thailand imposed an indefinite ban on electronic waste last summer, for example, while

Vietnam stopped issuing waste-import licenses and vowed to stop importing scrap plastic by 2025.

In the Philippines last week, officials returned a shipment of waste that had been mistakenly sent there from Canada several years ago, and vowed to send another back to Hong Kong.

"Load that up on a ship and I will advise Canada that your garbage is on the way," President Rodrigo Duterte of the Philippines said of the Canadian shipment in early May. "Prepare a grand reception. Eat it if you want to."

In Malaysia, the campaign against imported waste has been led by Yeo Bee Yin, the 36-year-old environment minister. On a trip last week to Port Klang, down the road from Telok Gong, she said the government would soon return 10 of about 60 containers with waste from the United States and elsewhere that had been smuggled into illegal processing facilities.

Ms. Yeo's campaign may be a way to score public relations points against countries, including the United States, that have criticized Malaysia for its high rates of deforestation and other severe environmental problems, said Helena Varkkey, an expert on pollution in Southeast Asia at the University of Malaya in Kuala Lumpur.

"This is a 'Here's a taste of your own medicine,' " she said. Ms. Yeo's office could not be reached for comment.

But whatever the motivation, one danger may be that legal recyclers across Southeast Asia will now miss a chance to both scale up their business and help mitigate environmental problems, including the scourge of plastics in the oceans.

Some plastic waste, if properly sorted and classified, is already being used in the region as a raw material for high-end manufacturing and as a replacement for fossil fuels in cement kilns, among other uses. And because municipal waste sorting here is virtually nonexistent, importing plastic scrap is often the only way for recycling companies to achieve economies of scale.

But the current waste crackdowns have not clearly distinguished between truly hazardous garbage and other types of plastic that can be safely recycled again and again, said Douglas Woodring, the founder of the Ocean Recovery Alliance, a nonprofit based in California and Hong Kong that works on plastic pollution.

"You're categorizing these as a dangerous substance, which they are not if you process them the right way," he said. "They're just like any other commodity — like copper, steel, metal, wood and paper."

Some recyclers are already feeling the effects. Officials in the Philippines, for example, declined to issue import permits last month for a shipment of plastic-waste-based fuel that is produced in Australia and used in the production of cement, customs paperwork shows.

In a report explaining the decision, a Philippine customs official noted that the import request had been rejected partly because of "past and present controversies on the importation of waste." He also said the shipment had emitted a "pungent smell inherent to municipal waste" upon inspection at a Philippine port.

Pavel Cech, the Malaysian-based managing director of ResourceCo Asia, the Southeast Asian branch of an Australian company that produces the fuel, said that between 100 and 150 shipping containers of it would not reach cement kilns in Malaysia and the Philippines this month because of customs disputes. He said the cement companies that use the fuel in their kilns would now burn coal instead.

Mr. Cech said he was pleading his case to officials but did not expect the region's governments to clarify their plastic scrap policies anytime soon.

"Throughout Southeast Asia," he said, "politics and populism prevails over a technocratic approach."

MUKTITA SUHARTONO contributed reporting from Bangkok, and **JASON GUTIERREZ** from Subic Bay in the Philippines.

Cleansing Plastic From Oceans: Big Ask for a Country That Loves Wrap

BY MOTOKO RICH | JUNE 27, 2019

OSAKA, JAPAN — Shoji Kousaka always thought of Japan as a place where people knew how to dispose of their trash.

That was before he spent a morning on a fishing trawler in Osaka Bay last fall, shocked by the reams of soda bottles, plastic shopping bags, snack wrappers and drinking straws repeatedly trapped in the nets, along with the flounder and shrimp.

"Things that weren't supposed to be there were there," said Mr. Kousaka, a deputy chief of the Union of Kansai Government, a regional federation representing the second-largest metropolitan area in Japan after Tokyo. Based on what he saw in six hours on the boat, Mr. Kousaka estimates more than 6.1 million plastic scraps and about 3 million plastic bags sit on the floor of the bay.

Given Japan's high collection rate for plastic waste and the country's rigorous approach to recycling, said Mr. Kousaka, "I was surprised at how much trash was at the bottom of the ocean."

As world leaders have been flying in for the Group of 20 summit meeting that officially opens on Friday in Osaka, they will be meeting in a conference center about a mile from the bay where Mr. Kousaka discovered the offending plastic.

Reducing the plastic waste that flows into the oceans is a critical proposal by Prime Minister Shinzo Abe of Japan as he hosts the G-20 meeting.

Single-use plastic bottles and utensils are banned from the international media center, and reporters received gift bags that included a cup made from recycled plastic, imprinted with a cartoon of a crying turtle paddling beside a floating water bottle, straw and grocery bag. "Let's protect the ocean from plastic waste!" reads the caption.

At a meeting of environment ministers this month in Karuizawa,

Japan, the group agreed on voluntary measures designed to study the problem and ultimately clean up. According to scientific estimates, the 20 countries generate about half of all marine plastic litter, which has the potential to destroy ecosystems, obstruct navigation and befoul beaches.

Critics have already assailed the measures for lacking any numerical reduction targets. But experts and advocates say the Group of 20 measures at least keep marine plastic waste in the public eye.

"It's useful in that it maintains the issue on the top of the international agenda," said Torbjorn Graff Hugo of the International Law and Policy Institute in Oslo, who has written about the need for an international treaty to control marine plastic waste. "And this group of countries is using the opportunity to reinforce their commitment to do something about this."

For Japan, the world's second-largest generator of plastic packaging waste per person behind the United States, the problem is more than proper disposal.

The Japanese are often praised for their meticulous trash collection — remember the World Cup soccer fans who cleaned up all their cups and wrappers before they left the stadium? — and can be extremely careful about separating waste for recycling.

But plastic consumption is deeply embedded in Japanese culture, where vegetables sold in grocery stores are individually wrapped, packages are often double-bagged and ubiquitous vending machines dispense plentiful plastic bottles.

While most municipalities have sophisticated collection systems — somewhere between 70 and 80 percent of used plastic wrappers, bottles and bags are collected by waste management companies and then recycled or incinerated — Japan's Environment Ministry estimates that between 20,000 and 60,000 tons of plastic waste end up in the ocean each year.

In talking about marine plastic litter, Mr. Abe has mainly pushed for improvements in trash collection and recycling rather than a substantial reduction in the total amount of plastic the Japanese use.

"We're not really tackling the source of the problem," said Karen Raubenheimer, a lecturer at the University of Wollongong in Australia and an expert in marine plastic policy. "If you're only talking about collection and waste management, you're not talking about reduction of production and consumption."

Chiyoko Yamada, 72, was shopping in a basement food court at the Kintetsu Department Store in Osaka on Thursday, her basket filled with plastic-swathed groceries. There were plastic food containers of fried soba noodles and savory pancakes known as okonomiyaki, filled with individual plastic sachets for each ingredient. A sole carrot sheathed in plastic wrap sat at the bottom of her basket next to four spears of asparagus, also wrapped in plastic.

"I think all that plastic is excessive," Ms. Yamada said. "It just creates a lot of work for me at home unwrapping every individual thing."

Ms. Yamada did not put much stock in the marine plastic initiative that Mr. Abe is promoting at the Group of 20 summit meeting. "I think that is just Abe talking," she said. "I don't think it will be effective."

Japan's track record on marine waste is mixed; at the Group of 7 meeting in Canada last year, it did not sign a plastics charter aimed at reducing marine waste. The only other country that did not sign was the United States.

Globally, one of the biggest problems is that developed nations offload their trash by exporting it to poorer countries that may not have sophisticated recycling systems.

"It's the big lie," Ms. Raubenheimer said. "Yes, we say we are recycling so much, but how much are we recycling domestically, and when we send it overseas, there is no way of tracking that."

Two years ago, China, which had been a major destination for exported waste, banned most plastic trash shipments. Now countries like Japan are shipping their plastic to countries in Southeast Asia. Because the recipients lack the capacity to recycle it all, more plastic waste ends up in the sea.

At the same time, developing countries are increasing their use of plastic, often as part of a program to improve food safety and hygiene.

Experts warn that the drive to reduce plastic use could pose risks to the health of citizens in poor countries.

"If all plastic is removed from the world, children may get more diseases from polluted dishes and forks," said Atsuhiko Isobe, a professor at the Research Institute for Applied Mechanics at Kyushu University, who has studied marine plastic waste.

He agrees with the goal of reducing plastic consumption, he said, but it should be done "step by step and in line with scientific evidence."

"Plastic has a risk to the natural environment," he said, "but simultaneously, removing plastic also has a risk to the world."

EIMI YAMAMITSU contributed research.

Beverage Companies Embrace Recycling, Until It Costs Them

BY MICHAEL CORKERY | JULY 4, 2019

They have pledged to help fix U.S. recycling, but for decades the companies have fought against "bottle bills," which result in more bottles and cans being recycled but are costly for the industry.

RECYCLING IS STRUGGLING in much of the United States, and companies like Coca-Cola say they are committed to fixing it.

The beverage industry helps pay for pizza parties celebrating top elementary school recyclers and lends money to companies that process used plastic. Coca-Cola and Pepsi, along with Dow, the plastics producer, support nonprofit groups like Keep America Beautiful, which organize events like litter cleanups. A recent video funded partly by Keep America Beautiful featured models dancing through a recycling facility in Brooklyn, which one advertising writer said makes "recycling sexy." By 2030, Coca-Cola wants all of its packaging to be made from at least 50 percent recycled content.

But one approach to recycling that many of these companies do not support has proved to actually work: container deposit laws, more commonly known as bottle bills, which cost them lots of money.

In the 10 states where consumers can collect a few cents when they return an empty bottle or can, recycling rates for those containers are often significantly higher. In some cases, they are more than twice as high as in states without such deposits.

For decades, beverage companies, retailers and many of the nonprofit groups they control have fought to kill bottle bill proposals across the country — with great success. Since 1987, only one state, Hawaii, has passed a bottle bill. This year, such measures have been proposed in at least eight states. Nearly all have been rejected or failed to gain traction.

Plastic bottles are sorted out from other materials in Hickman County, Tenn., May 14, 2019.

The result? Recycling in much of the country still depends almost entirely on the good will of consumers to place their used containers in a bin for pickup. The process is convenient, but means millions of bottles and cans head straight to a dump instead.

The financial reason for such opposition is clear. If the other 40 states were to adopt expansive bottle bills, it could ultimately cost the industries billions more. The beverage industry says the bills function like a tax and allow governments to collect millions in unclaimed deposits. Beverage distributors, in many cases, also pay a handling fee for the processing of empty containers.

"I am confident that the industry's true rationale for opposing deposit laws is that they cost them money and they don't want the expense," said Susan Collins, president of the Container Recycling Institute, a research and advocacy group that supports bottle bills.

Most recently, in Connecticut last month, the industry helped to soundly defeat a bill that would have expanded deposits to juice and energy drink bottles, along with soda and beer.

"It's like Groundhog Day all over again," Chris Phelps, state director of the advocacy group Environment Connecticut, told a local newspaper shortly after the measure was defeated in the state legislature. "Every year when it comes to the bottle bill, every year, no progress is made, despite a lot of effort, a lot of work, a lot of recognition of the need to make progress."

Facing public pressure over its contribution to plastic pollution in the ocean and the problems with many municipal recycling systems, the beverage industry has released broad statements in recent weeks suggesting a new openness to bottle bills.

In response to questions from The New York Times about the industry's lobbying efforts, the American Beverage Association said in an email that while it had opposed bottle bills "in the past," it was "open to any ideas" that would create more recycled plastic.

"This includes a deposit or fee on our containers," the trade group said.

The industry argues that bottle bills address only one source of plastic waste — soda and water bottles. Beverage companies and retailers say they want to increase recycling rates for all types of plastic, including yogurt containers and food pouches that would be excluded from deposit laws.

Bottle bill supporters acknowledge that the systems have flaws, but blame retailers and bottlers for opposing attempts to modernize them.

"It gets to the larger question about recycling as a whole," said Darryl Young, a former board member of the National Recycling Coalition. "Is it really just a way for manufacturers to avoid responsibility for their waste?"

Years ago, the National Recycling Coalition considered merging with Keep America Beautiful. Mr. Young said he voted down the deal partly because of concerns about the agenda of the group's corporate donors.

"They want to help," Mr. Young said, "but on their own terms."

'LET THAT DOG LIE'

Laura Turner Seydel, an environmental advocate and daughter of the media mogul Ted Turner, started a group called Atlanta Recycles in 2005 after learning about what seemed like an absurd conundrum.

Recycling rates in Georgia were so low that local carpet manufacturers, a large user of recycled plastic, were forced to import the material from outside the state, even though Atlanta is home to the headquarters of Coca-Cola, one of the world's largest producers of plastic bottles.

This winter, Ms. Seydel said, she witnessed why, 14 years after she founded Atlanta Recycles, little has changed.

"It exemplified why the wheels are coming off recycling," she said.

In January, some members of the group — made up of business leaders, government officials and environmentalists — were briefed on a $4 million investment that the Coca-Cola Foundation was making in the city. Coca-Cola, the group learned, had chosen Atlanta to showcase its "World Without Waste" campaign, which centered on increasing collection rates of bottles and cans.

The company, through a group called the Recycling Partnership, would pay for city workers to comb through residential recycling bins and leave behind "inspirational scorecards" marking which items could be recycled and which belonged in the trash. The program had been tested successfully on a smaller scale.

Someone in the meeting floated another idea: Why not explore the idea of a bottle bill in Georgia?

The proposal was quickly shot down. Several members of the group expressed concern that pushing for a bottle bill could jeopardize the funding from Coca-Cola. The message, Ms. Seydel recalled, was "you better let that dog lie." The discussion at the meeting grew heated.

Ms. Seydel and others argued that bottle bills were proven methods to increase collection rates of used plastic.

Kanika Greenlee, the city's environmental programs director, had come prepared with a statement from Coca-Cola, making clear its opposition to deposits. Bottle bills were inconvenient and costly, the company said.

Ms. Greenlee, who through a spokeswoman declined to comment, holds several roles related to recycling in Atlanta. She works in the city's public works department, but she also serves on the national board of directors of Keep America Beautiful alongside executives from Coca-Cola, Dr Pepper, Pepsi and the American Chemistry Council, a trade group for chemical and plastics companies.

A spokesman for Keep America Beautiful, which the packaging industry helped create in 1953 to combat litter, said the group had a "neutral" position on bottle bills and that "all options at this point need to be on the table" to improve recycling.

In a statement, Coca-Cola said company policy positions were independent of its foundation's donations, adding that the grant had already been awarded when the Atlanta Recycles meeting took place.

"We are open to exploring a variety of strategies to achieve our goal of recovering and recycling the equivalent of a bottle or can for every one we sell by 2030," Coca-Cola said, adding that it found curbside recycling was "one of the most effective and convenient recycling solutions for consumers."

'A SUPERIOR STRATEGY'

Empty bottles have vexed the beverage industry for more than a century. They are "the monstrous evil that saps the life from an otherwise prosperous trade," The National Bottlers Gazette wrote in 1882.

Back then, beverage companies desperately wanted their bottles back because the glass containers were so expensive to make. The companies even conducted raids on homes to retrieve their used containers from housewives who used them to store ketchup and medicine.

By the 1980s, however, mass-produced plastic made bottles inexpensive — and people rarely reused them. They often ended up being tossed on the side of the road, and the beverage companies simply made more of them.

Bottle bills were passed partly in an effort to reduce this kind of litter. But states like Tennessee, New Jersey and Washington settled on an alternative. In Tennessee, beverage companies agreed to pay a small tax in order to fund litter pickup efforts, education programs and handouts promoting recycling.

There was another bonus. In many parts of the state, inmates would perform the daily litter cleanup, keeping costs low and rewarding good behavior in the county jails. The tax revenue pays for salaries and other expenses of county sheriffs overseeing the litter crews, like lunch from McDonald's for the inmates.

"It makes the time go easier," one inmate, Miko Coleman, 29, said as he picked up trash along a quiet country road this spring.

But the money — and the cleanup crews — would go away if Tennessee enacted a bottle bill, according to a provision in the law. That has made it difficult for bottle bills to gain traction politically.

"I have to hand it to the industry, they have a superior strategy," said Marge Davis, a writer and conservationist, who has been proposing a bottle bill in Tennessee nearly every year since 2004.

Ms. Davis says the litter pickup helps to beautify roads, but does not get at the core issue of recycling more bottles and cans. And even though her bottle bill proposal would find a new funding source for roadside cleanups, she has had a hard time convincing lawmakers.

At times, Ms. Davis' efforts faced another opponent — the group Keep Tennessee Beautiful. Like the work crews, Keep Tennessee Beautiful derives much of its funding from the tax money.

Keep Tennessee Beautiful's organizational values, according to its website, include "personal responsibility" and "policy based on fact."

For several years, the group circulated research and spoke out against bottle bills. Their argument, presented in a two-page white paper in 2002, mirrored the beverage industry's position closely. Stopping litter and encouraging recycling are best done through education, it said, not through 5-cent deposits.

"Funds should go for prevention education," the white paper states. "Teach the child and retrain the adult."

Missy Marshall, who has been executive director of Keep Tennessee Beautiful since 2013, said her group does not currently have an official position on deposits, but she worries about upending funding for a system that is successfully reducing litter.

"What we don't think is a positive step is to undo what we are doing," she said.

LOBBYING POWER UNLEASHED

One of the industry's chief criticisms of bottle bills is that they deprive municipal recycling programs of valuable scrap material like aluminum cans. Selling this material helps offset the cost of processing items that are less valuable.

This argument has gained particular credence among environmental groups and municipalities after China put strict limits on the amount of plastic scraps that it imports from the United States. The policy shift in China led to a glut of used plastic and paper around the country, forcing some communities to burn or bury material they cannot offload.

In Washington State, Sen. Christine Rolfes thought she had come up with a comprehensive solution. This winter, Ms. Rolfes introduced a bill that she said was intended to hold all plastic packaging manufacturers responsible for the recycling of not just plastic soda and water bottles, but also harder-to-process plastics like takeout containers and packaging wrap.

Representatives of roughly 20 companies and trade groups testified against the bill, including a group called the American Institute for Packaging and the Environment, whose members, according to its website, include ExxonMobil's chemical division and Pepsico.

"They pretty much represented the entire economy," Ms. Rolfes said of the bill's many opponents. "It was insidious."

After several revisions, the current version of the bill no longer holds plastic manufacturers responsible for recycling.

The bill, which has been signed into law, now directs a state agency to study different approaches to recycling plastic packaging. The report is due by October 2020.

MICHAEL CORKERY is a business reporter who covers the retail industry and its impact on consumers, workers and the economy. He joined The Times in 2014 and was previously a reporter at the Wall Street Journal and the Providence Journal.

Are Mini Shampoo Bottles the New Plastic Straw?

BY ELAINE GLUSAC | JULY 29, 2019

The IHG hotel group plans to replace "bathroom miniatures" with bulk supplies across all of its 17 brands, including Holiday Inn and InterContinental, becoming the first big brand to act.

NOW THAT THE hotel industry has largely embraced bans on plastic straws, one major hotel group aims to eliminate the next set of plastic targets: mini bottles of shampoo, conditioner, lotion and the like.

On Tuesday, July 30, IHG will announce it plans to replace all "bathroom miniatures" with bulk supplies across all of its 17 brands, including Holiday Inn Hotels and Resorts and InterContinental Hotels & Resorts. The decision will affect 843,000 guest rooms in more than 5,600 hotels during 2021.

"Today's customers and colleagues expect us to have less impact on the environment," said Keith Barr, the chief executive of IHG. He called the company's plastic straw ban, which was announced in October 2018, to be a first step in a wider sustainability program. "This, to me, was the next logical step."

While IHG is the first company to issue the brand-wide ban, many hotels already use refillable dispensers of personal care products, often associated with affordable hotels, rather than single-use items.

"Budget hotels have always been more likely to have bulk shampoo and conditioner dispensers in the shower, and some also have them by the sink. The reason is cost," said Henry H. Harteveldt, a travel industry analyst and the president of Atmosphere Research Group. "It costs them less to install and service these bulk dispensers than providing individual cakes of soap and bottles of shampoo, conditioner and the like."

Mr. Barr acknowledged the savings in costs to hotel operations, but framed it as a win-win that, "makes environmental and commercial sense," he said.

The hurdle may be convincing an InterContinental guest to accept a bulk dispenser in the bath as better than the mini bottle of high-end shampoo. Some luxury travel companies have been moving in that direction. The luxury cruise line Lindblad Expeditions uses refillable dispensers for soap, shampoo and other liquid products on all of its ships, including the upcoming National Geographic Endurance, launching in April 2020. The Waldorf Astoria Maldives Ithaafushi, which opened July 1, offers Salvatore Ferragamo bathroom amenities in refillable marble containers. In Namibia, andBeyond Sossusvlei Desert Lodge, opening in October, plans to put bath products in bulk glass bottles.

Several IHG brands already offer bulk bathroom amenities, including the high-end Six Senses Hotels Resorts Spas, which IHG acquired earlier this year, where bathrooms are fitted with refillable ceramic dispensers. It also furnishes bathroom products in bulk at its wellness-centered Even, mid-scale Avid and new upscale Voco hotels.

The mini bottle ban is the latest salvo in an escalating battle against plastic waste. Municipalities and companies are making moves — like San Francisco's initiative to ban the sale of plastic water bottles on city property and IKEA's commitment to ditch single-use plastic plates, cups and cutlery in its houseware lines and in-store cafes. In the travel industry, major hotel groups, including Marriott International and Hilton, have pledged to rid their properties of plastic straws. Airlines including American, Delta and United have done the same in their airplanes.

Following IHG's move to ban personal products in mini plastic bottles, others may be forced to follow. The California Legislature is currently considering Assembly Bill 1162, which would prohibit hotels, beginning in 2023, from providing miniature plastic bottles of personal care products.

According to the World Bank, some 242 million tons of plastic waste was produced in 2016 and this waste is projected to grow to 3.4 billion tons in 2050. The World Economic Forum found at least 8 million tons of plastics end up in the ocean annually, and that only 14 percent of plastic packaging material globally is collected for recycling.

To Mr. Barr, the green swap is worth any disappointment on the part of travelers who may miss taking home their freebie bottles of Agraria shampoo from an InterContinental resort or Beekman 1802 lotion from a Crowne Plaza hotel.

"I'm sure I will get some emails from some customers, but I'm betting I'll get more thank you's for taking a step forward and having a positive effect on the environment," he said.

A Giant Factory Rises to Make a Product Filling Up the World: Plastic

BY MICHAEL CORKERY | AUG. 12, 2019

Royal Dutch Shell's plant will produce more than a million tons of plastic, in the form of tiny pellets. Many in the Pittsburgh area see it as an economic engine, but others worry about long-term harm.

MONACA, PA. — The 386-acre property looks like a giant Lego set rising from the banks of the Ohio River. It is one of the largest active construction projects in the United States, employing more than 5,000 people.

When completed, the facility will be fed by pipelines stretching hundreds of miles across Appalachia. It will have its own rail system with 3,300 freight cars. And it will produce more than a million tons each year of something that many people argue the world needs less of: plastic.

As concern grows about plastic debris in the oceans and recycling continues to falter in the United States, the production of new plastic is booming. The plant that Royal Dutch Shell is building about 25 miles northwest of Pittsburgh will create tiny pellets that can be turned into items like phone cases, auto parts and food packaging, all of which will be around long after they have served their purpose.

The plant is one of more than a dozen that are being built or have been proposed around the world by petrochemical companies like Exxon Mobil and Dow, including several in nearby Ohio and West Virginia and on the Gulf Coast. And after decades of seeing American industrial jobs head overseas, the rise of the petrochemical sector is creating excitement. On Tuesday, President Trump is scheduled to tour the Shell plant.

"Where we are coming from is that plastic, in most of its forms, is good and it serves to be good for humanity," said Hilary Mercer, who is overseeing the construction project for Shell.

Samples of the plastic pellets that Shell will produce with its ethane cracker plant in Beaver County, Pa.

The boom is driven partly by plastic's popularity as a versatile and inexpensive material that keeps potato chips fresh and makes cars lighter. But in parts of the Appalachian region, the increase is also being fueled by an overabundance of natural gas.

It has been about 15 years since hydraulic fracturing, or fracking, took hold in Pennsylvania, which sits atop the huge gas reserve of the Marcellus Shale. But natural gas prices have collapsed and profit must be found elsewhere, namely the natural gas byproduct ethane, which is unleashed during fracking and can be made into polyethylene, a common form of plastic.

This is a place where, right now, plastic makes sense to many people. To the labor union gaining new members. To the world's third-largest company struggling with low oil prices. And to the former government officials who, in seeking to create jobs, offered Shell one of the largest tax breaks in state history.

But any short-term good could have long-term costs.

Shell says much of the plastic from the plant can be used to create fuel-efficient cars and medical devices. But the industry acknowledges that some of the world's waste management systems are unable to keep up with other forms of plastic like water bottles, grocery bags and food containers being discarded by consumers on the move.

Studies have detected plastic fibers everywhere — in the stomachs of sperm whales, in tap water and in table salt. A researcher in Britain says plastic may help define the most recent layer of the earth's crust because it takes so long to break down and there is so much of it.

"Plastic really doesn't go away," said Roland Geyer, a professor of industrial ecology at the University of California, Santa Barbara. "It just accumulates and ends up in the wrong places. And we just don't know the long-term implications of having all this plastic everywhere in the natural environment. It is like this giant global experiment and we can't just pull the plug if it goes wrong."

'PART OF A JOURNEY'

The roots of Shell's sleek, ultramodern plant date back hundreds of millions of years, when the area was occupied by a wide inland sea.

Over time, the earth shifted and the sea was covered by rock, which compressed all of the dead organisms and sediment that had settled on its watery bottom into rich layers of hydrocarbons, including those that make up natural gas.

Ms. Mercer has spent 32 years traveling the world for Shell — in southern Iraq and in eastern Russia — helping turn those hydrocarbons deep within the earth into energy. These days, Ms. Mercer, an English-born, Oxford-educated engineer, works out of a red brick building in Beaver, Pa.

The plant Ms. Mercer has come here to build is "as big as you get," she said. When finished, Shell's cracker plant — named for the chemical reaction of "cracking" gas molecules into the building blocks of plastic — will consume vast quantities of ethane pumped from wells across Pennsylvania into an enormous furnace. The superheated gas is then cooled, forming solid pellets about the size of arborio rice. The process takes about 20 hours.

In Ms. Mercer's view, this is a positive development for the environment. Creating more plastic, she says, helps to reduce carbon emissions by creating lighter and more efficient cars and airplanes. "You have plastic in wind turbines. You have plastic in solar panels."

She added: "The ability to do those renewable things relies to some extent on the plastics we produce and the chemicals that we produce. I don't see a contradiction. I see it as part of a journey."

Shell's journey into plastics was driven by a need to generate profits at a time its primary business — oil and gas production — struggles with persistently low prices. It is also a way for the energy industry to hedge against declining gasoline consumption as cars become more efficient or powered by electricity.

A big demand for plastic comes from auto manufacturers and for consumer packaging like the ones displayed in a mock grocery store in the lobby of Shell's Pennsylvania offices: plastic cups, diapers and paper towel rolls wrapped in plastic.

There's also a stack of brochures in the lobby titled the Shell Polymers "Constitution" that reads: "We are called to Beaver Valley by the desire to be part of something larger than ourselves — to leave a legacy of care, innovation and success for future generations."

Ms. Mercer said the problem with plastic is not its production, but when it is improperly disposed. "We passionately believe in recycling." she said.

Shell is involved in a broad industry effort to clean up the world's largest sources of plastic waste. And in Beaver County, Shell recently donated money to extend the hours of the local recycling center and it supports other initiatives that the company believes will contribute to a "circular economy."

But a circular economy has not yet taken hold in Beaver. Like many areas around the country, the county has had to limit the type of plastic packaging it can accept for recycling because there are relatively few buyers who want to repurpose it.

"We are looking for long-term solutions right now," a spokeswoman for the recycling center said.

'THIS IS WHERE YOU WANT TO BE'

It was a golden autumn afternoon in Pittsburgh, sunny and mild. The Steelers were in town playing at Heinz Field, and Gov. Tom Corbett got two box-seat tickets to the game.

The governor's guest at the game in October 2012 was a Shell executive, who was helping to decide where the company would locate its giant cracker plant. Mr. Corbett took the executive down to the field to meet some of the players. Then the governor walked him out to midfield to stand on the Steelers' yellow and black logo.

"I told him, 'This is where you want to be,' " Mr. Corbett recalled.

Shell agreed, and was offered a tax break that was projected to save the company an estimated $1.6 billion.

Mr. Corbett, a Republican, said the plastics plant would bolster communities in an area devastated by the collapse of the steel industry in the 1980s, when the unemployment rate hit 28 percent.

"Did you know there is a Steelers bar in Rome?" Mr. Corbett asked in a phone interview. "The reason the Steelers travel so well is because when steel died many people moved away."

Mr. Corbett said he believed the Shell plant was only the beginning of the state's plastics boom. He envisions manufacturers coming to Beaver County to be closer to the source of the raw plastic. His successor, Tom Wolf, a Democrat, has been courting more petrochemical development.

"We are rebuilding the economy," said Mr. Corbett, who left office in 2015 after one term.

Plastics is also solving a challenge for the state's fracking industry. The western part of the Marcellus Shale produces not just methane gas that is used for heating homes and cooking, but also so-called wet gases like ethane.

Ethane has a higher energy level, measured in British thermal units, or B.T.U.s, than methane. There are regulatory limits on how many B.T.U.s can be safely used in homes and businesses. So, much of the ethane is stripped out of the gas before the methane is shipped. Plastic production is one of the few viable uses for the ethane, and without it some fracking executives say they would not be able to operate many of their wells.

"What became apparent to me and the governor is that there needed to be an outlet for the ethane," said Patrick Henderson, Mr. Corbett's top energy adviser. He helped persuade the legislature to approve the tax credit, which will benefit Shell and any other petrochemical company that agrees to buy locally produced ethane and create a certain number of jobs.

Mr. Henderson now works on the government affairs team at the Marcellus Shale Coalition, which represents the state's fracking industry.

When burned, natural gas emits less carbon than oil and coal, but some people worry that it is preventing the widespread adoption of renewable energy sources and that gas production will only be increased.

The cracker plant itself is allowed by the state to emit 2.2 million tons of carbon dioxide each year, which is the equivalent of about 480,000 cars. Shell says the plant is likely to emit less than that.

"Will you eventually see everything renewable? Probably in 100 years," Mr. Corbett said. "But right now natural gas is giving a future to your grandchildren."

'WHAT IS LIFE GOING TO BE LIKE'

Around Beaver County, the cracker plant is creating opportunities for some and deep concerns for others.

Kristin Stanzak is the owner of Don's Deli in downtown Beaver, which she opened with her husband in 2016, just before construction of the Shell plant took off. On many afternoons, Ms. Stanzak runs out of sub rolls largely because of the orders from Shell — as many as 100 orders a day.

When that happens, she posts a picture of herself on Instagram dressed as Little Orphan Annie that reassures: "The subs will be back tomorrow! Betchyer bottom dollar that tomorrow … we'll have suuuubsss."

At the local union hall of the International Brotherhood of Electrical Workers, Larry Nelson oversees about 380 electricians working on the plant, including many who have relocated from 28 states. After decades of decline, union membership is growing again.

"The guys are tickled pink to be working on this thing," Mr. Nelson said.

But there will be only about 600 permanent jobs at the plant, about 12 percent of the construction workers at the site now. A company spokesman said the plant was expected to open "in the early 2020s."

Some residents say their worries about the cracker plant and fracking over the long term are already coming to bear. The impact of climate change, for example, can be seen around Beaver County, and at the plastics plant in particular.

This spring, the huge furnace that will heat the ethane was being shipped on the Mississippi River, but had difficulty fitting under some bridges because the water was so high from flooding. At the construction site, Shell has installed giant tarps to keep the workers dry in the frequent rain, which hit a record last year in Pittsburgh.

Some residents see other signs of trouble. At a community meeting Shell held in late June, Barbara Goblick quizzed a company representative about the safety of its pipelines that will feed ethane to the plant.

Ms. Goblick explained that she lives in a neighborhood, about two miles from the plant, where a pipeline exploded in September. The fire incinerated a nearby house, and the blast cracked walls and ceilings in Ms. Goblick's home. A landslide, partly caused by heavy rains, is believed to have set off the explosion.

The damaged pipeline was not operated by Shell, but a new ethane pipeline is being installed about 800 feet from her house.

"I worry it could happen again," she said.

Amanda Miller never paid much attention to the cracker plant rising 16 miles from her home in Franklin Park, an affluent suburb.

What made her speak out at a municipal meeting in January was a proposal by a fracking company to drill under a local park with hiking trails and playing fields.

"That was going too far," said Ms. Miller, an occupational therapist at a children's hospital in Pittsburgh.

The company's proposal was rebuffed. But it has leases on private land in the area that is rich in ethane.

The morning after the meeting, Ms. Miller woke up early to feed her 14-month-old daughter. Her other three children were still asleep. They had just celebrated her husband's grandmother's 99th birthday. In that quiet moment, alone with her daughter, Ms. Miller thought of the plastics plant and the fracking that was increasing around her.

"That's when it hit me," she said. "I looked at her and wondered what is life going to be like when she is 99. And for the first time I wasn't hopeful. I actually started to cry."

MICHAEL CORKERY is a business reporter who covers the retail industry and its impact on consumers, workers and the economy. He joined The Times in 2014 and was previously a reporter at the Wall Street Journal and the Providence Journal.

CHAPTER 4

A Future Without Plastic?

Where do we go from here? It is difficult to imagine a world without plastic, but these articles posit alternatives for a greener and healthier future. Including advice for limiting daily plastic usage and an accounting of recycling efforts across the globe, this chapter offers a more hopeful perspective on a possible path back to natural materials. Yet it remains clear that only a swift and dramatic change in our reliance on plastics, and disposal of synthetic materials, can encourage this kind of progress.

Raising Awareness of Plastic Waste

COLUMN | BY BETTINA WASSENER | AUG. 14, 2011

HONG KONG — Most people are familiar with the concept of a carbon footprint. Many may also know there is such a thing as a water footprint. But whoever heard of a plastic footprint? Well, soon, more and more people will have.

Starting in early October, hundreds of companies and institutions around the world will receive a questionnaire asking them to assess and report their use of plastic: how much they use, what processes they have for recycling and what — if any — policies they have to reduce their plastic consumption or to increase the proportion of recycled or biodegradable plastic within their organizations.

Fairly simple questions, but ones that could help to thrust the issue of plastic waste and pollution onto the radars of corporations, investors and the public in a much bigger way.

"What we're trying to do is to have companies manage and use plastic much more wisely, and to receive recognition for doing so from both customers and investors," said Doug Woodring, an environmental entrepreneur in Hong Kong who has a background in asset management and is the driving force behind the initiative.

"Plastic pollution is a major global phenomenon that has crept up on us over the decades, and it really requires a global and comprehensive solution that includes systemic rethinks about usage and production."

Announced last year, and due to be introduced formally in September, the Plastic Disclosure Project is trying to provide the solution that Mr. Woodring describes, by pushing the thinking about plastic pollution far beyond beach cleanups with an attempt to change the awareness and behavior of big users of plastic, which include not only companies but also universities, hospitals and sports groups.

The concept behind the project is not new. The initiative models itself on the Carbon Disclosure Project, which has been prodding companies into monitoring and improving their carbon emissions for about a decade.

About 3,000 organizations in about 60 countries measure and disclose their greenhouse gas emissions and climate change strategies through the carbon disclosure project. Last year, the project also began asking companies about their water use, with the same aim of prompting more conservative use of that resource.

Like the carbon project, the plastic disclosure initiative is backed by investors: asset managers who value information about any potential wastage or liabilities related to the use of energy, water or plastic, or, conversely, any improvements that will bolster a company's bottom line or its image with consumers.

"Increased transparency by companies should improve the ability of sustainable investors to assess the investment risks and opportunities of companies in the global plastic value chain," said Jeremy Higgs, managing director of Environmental Investment Services Asia, an investment management company in Hong Kong that last month became a founding sponsor of the Plastic Disclosure Project, with a $50,000 grant.

While carbon emissions and water use are pretty firmly embedded in the consciousness of most organizations, the use of plastic generally is not.

But campaigners and scientists are increasingly sounding the alarm over the amount of plastic that is used wastefully (think of single-use drink bottles and packaging), or that ends up as trash in rivers and oceans. Many say that plastic pollution has swelled into a major threat for the world's oceans and for the global environment as a whole.

The U.S. National Oceanic and Atmospheric Administration, for one, has said that marine debris "has become one of the most pervasive pollution problems facing the world's oceans and waterways."

And in Europe, the E.U. commissioner for maritime affairs and fisheries, Maria Damanaki, has said that pollution in the Mediterranean Sea has reached "alarming proportions."

Here is why: About 300 million tons of plastic is produced globally each year. Only about 10 percent of that is recycled. Of the plastic that is simply trashed, an estimated seven million tons ends up in the sea each year.

There, it breaks down into smaller and smaller fragments over the years.

The tinier the pieces, the more easily they are swallowed by marine life. (One study found that fish in the North Pacific ingest as much as 24,000 tons of plastic debris a year).

Because much of the disintegrating mass is no longer in the form of solid chunks, it is hard to scoop it out once it gets into the ocean. And because no single nation or authority bears responsibility for the oceans, cleanup and prevention are largely left to nongovernmental organizations.

"It's ironic: the very features that make plastic so popular also make it problematic," said Erik Floyd, a former equity analyst who is the treasurer of the Association for Sustainable and Responsible Investment in Asia and who co-founded the plastic project with Mr. Woodring.

In other words, because plastic is inexpensive, lightweight and durable, virtually every industry — be it retailing, manufacturing or logistics — loves it.

But because it is light and cheap, there is a lot of it. And because it is so durable, it does not "go away." Plastic accumulated over half a century is now out there.

A big part of the solution therefore has to be to prevent plastic from getting into the environment in the first place. That, in essence, is what the plastic disclosure project's team and its backers (it also has a stamp of approval from the Clinton Global Initiative) are trying to do.

By getting companies to assess their own — and their suppliers' and service providers' — plastic footprints voluntarily, the project is hoping to raise awareness of the problem and the potential savings that can be made, and to prompt organizations to change their consumption patterns.

That could mean reducing wasteful use; collecting, reusing or recycling plastic trash; stepping up the use of recycled plastic or of more easily biodegradable materials; and modifying product designs to minimize plastic use. The information compiled could be valuable to investors.

Some companies have already made progress on those fronts. Electrolux, the Swedish appliance maker, for example, introduced a range of vacuum cleaners in February that are made from recycled plastic. Coca-Cola has devised a plastic bottle that also contains plant-based materials. And Procter & Gamble has the long-term aim of using 100 percent recycled or renewable material in its products and packaging.

"Once you've taken an inventory of your use for the first time, it's easy to improve on it," said Mr. Woodring. "It's not necessarily painful."

Further down the line, the time may come when plastic trash is seen as something that has greater commercial value. After all, plastic, which is petroleum-based, can be converted into fuel. The technologies to do so exist, but "trash-to-cash" projects are mostly still small because the recycling and collection programs needed to give them a reliable supply of plastic waste are insufficient or completely absent.

With any luck, the plastic project will help start more action on that front, too.

Is It Time to Bag the Plastic?

ANALYSIS | BY ELISABETH ROSENTHAL | MAY 18, 2013

IN MY NEW YORK CITY apartment, the kitchen drawers, the coat closet, even the wine rack are overflowing with a type of waste that is rapidly disappearing elsewhere — the used plastic shopping bag.

Many countries and a handful of American cities have more or less done away with this supposed convenience item, by discouraging its use through plastic-bag taxes at checkout counters or outright bans. Walk down the streets of Dublin or Seattle or San Francisco and there is barely a bag in sight. Life continues.

"It didn't take people very long to accommodate at all," said Dick Lilly, manager for waste prevention in Seattle, where a plastic-bag ban took effect last summer. "Basically overnight those grocery and drug-store bags were gone."

But in much of America we seem more addicted than ever. On a recent shopping trip to Target in Chicago for some dorm supplies while visiting my son, I emerged with what seemed to be more bags than socks or rolls of toilet paper (only a slight exaggeration). At my local supermarket, plastic bags are applied layer upon layer around purchases, like Russian nesting dolls.

"Plastic shopping bags are an enormous problem for New York City," said Ron Gonen, the deputy commissioner of sanitation for recycling and waste reduction, noting that the city pays $10 million annually to send 100,000 tons of plastic bags that are tossed in the general trash to landfills in South Carolina, Ohio and Pennsylvania. That, he points out, "is amazing to think of, because a plastic bag doesn't weigh much at all."

All across the country, plastic bags are the bane of recycling programs. When carelessly placed into recycling bins for general plastic — which they often are — the bags jam and damage expensive sorting machines, which cost huge amounts to repair.

"We have to get people to start carrying reusable bags," Mr. Gonen said. "We're going to do what we can to start moving the needle."

"The question," he continued, "is do we use a carrot or a stick to change behavior?"

So far New York has used carrots, to little effect. (More about that later.) Unfortunately, most experts believe it will take a stiff stick to break a habit as ingrained as this one is in the United States. (In many European countries, like France and Italy, the plastic bag thing never fully caught on.)

In my case, I know I should bring a cloth bag along for shopping trips. And I do — when I remember. But experience shows that even environmentally conscious people need prodding and incentives to change their behavior permanently.

Where they exist, bans and charges or taxes (when set high enough) have been extremely successful and often raise revenue for other environmental projects. Unfortunately, these tactics are deeply unpopular in most of the nation.

After Austin, Tex., passed a bag ban earlier this year and with Dallas considering one, State Representative Drew Springer, a Republican, introduced the Shopping Bag Freedom Act in the Legislature. That act essentially bans bag bans, protecting the right of merchants to provide bags of any material to customers.

Businesses often fight hard against plastic-bag laws. When in 2007, Seattle first tried to impose a fee of 20 cents for each plastic bag, the American Chemistry Council financed a popular referendum that voted down the "bag tax," before it even took effect, Mr. Lilly said.

It took several more years for the city to regroup and impose its current ban. Plastic shopping bags are forbidden in stores, and though paper bags may be used, each one costs the shopper 5 cents. (There are exemptions, however: restaurants managed to secure one for takeout food, for example.)

A number of states are considering some form of statewide bans or taxes. And last month, Representative James P. Moran, Democrat of Virginia, introduced a bill to create a national 5-cent tax on all disposable plastic or paper bags provided by stores to customers. Some of the revenue would be used to create a Disposable Carryout Bag Trust Fund and to maintain national parks.

Actually, the idea of a bag tax may not seem so foreign to federal lawmakers: for the past three years, Washington has had its own 5-cent tax. Although bag use there dropped sharply, many experts feel that the charge should be even higher. In Ireland, for example, the bag tax is about 30 cents per bag.

By any measure, New Yorkers are laggards on the issue. In 2008, Mayor Michael R. Bloomberg tried unsuccessfully to pass a bag tax of 6 cents. More recently, New York State has preferred to attack the problem with soft diplomacy. Since 2009, large stores throughout the state providing plastic bags have been required to take them back for recycling. But there is not much enforcement, Mr. Gonen said, and the program "hasn't put a dent" in the numbers.

While the chain pharmacies and supermarkets in my neighborhood initially put out recycling bins for the bags, they have largely disappeared. Some stores will begrudgingly take back plastic at the sales counter — though I've seen the bags subsequently tossed in the trash. (Though plastic bags can be recycled, they must be separated from other forms of plastic.) The Bloomberg administration is also considering partnering with supermarkets to create incentive programs with shopping points awarded to those who bring reusable bags.

Frank Convery, an economist at University College, Dublin, who has studied the effects of Ireland's 10-year-old bag tax — the first in the world — is skeptical: "As regards the plastic bag issue, whatever is done has to be mandatory," he said. "The New York model is designed to fail."

Mr. Gonen said cities got a lot of complaints about plastic bags. So why wouldn't that inspire more of them to take action? It is another paradox of environmental politics — just as when New Yorkers show strong support for a bike-sharing plan but protest when bike-sharing racks appear on their sidewalk.

In a city where dog owners are forced to pick up their pets' waste and are precluded from smoking in parks, why is it so hard to get people to employ reusable bags for shopping?

ELISABETH ROSENTHAL is a reporter on the environment and health for The New York Times.

Let's Bag Plastic Bags

OPINION | BY JOSEPH CURTIN | MARCH 3, 2018

ALL IT HAD TAKEN was a moment's distraction. In a well-practiced sleight of hand, the cashier had double-bagged in plastic a dozen eggs, which were already encased in two protective layers of plastic. I briefly contemplated appealing for the liberation of my groceries but chose the path of least resistance. The deed was done, and the purveyors of plastic had been victorious on this occasion.

It was not always thus. In the late 1970s, single-use plastic bags were seldom available in grocery stores. Since then they have become an omnipresent part of the exchange of merchandise for money, a "free" offering to consecrate the ritual. An estimated one trillion bags are used each year globally, but they are so seamlessly ingrained into our daily routines that we hardly notice. It is difficult to imagine life without them.

The average American throws away about 10 single-use plastic bags per week, but New Yorkers use twice the national average. Some 23 billion are used across the state each year — more than enough, when tied together, to stretch to the moon and back 13 times. In the short trip from store to home the utility of these bags is spent, but the bags themselves can take millions of times longer to break down in landfill.

Yes, you are correct. This is crazy and entirely unnecessary. In Ireland, my home country, plastic bags were once an essential part of daily life. They were often found polluting waterways and littering the countryside, fluttering in trees and hedges. After a 15 euro cent fee was introduced in 2002, however, annual use dropped from an estimated 328 to 14 per person by 2014. Within a year of the fee's imposition, a national survey found that 90 percent of shoppers were using reusable bags; litter had also been reduced significantly.

Other countries have followed suit, though in a trickle, not a flood. But now political momentum is gathering across the globe to address

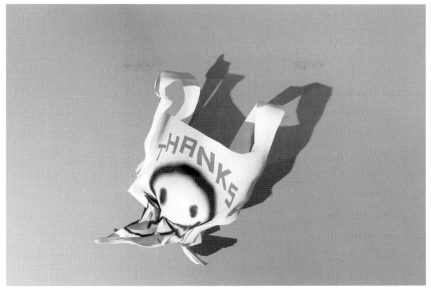

the problems that plastics pose for the planet. Last year, Kenya banned plastic bags, becoming the latest of more than two dozen countries to either prohibit them or impose a fee for their use.

In the United States, California is the only state to have imposed a comprehensive solution to the plastic bag problem, banning single-use plastic bags in stores in 2014, an action then endorsed by voters in a statewide referendum in 2016. Dozens of municipalities have banned plastic bags or imposed fees to discourage their use, including Austin, Tex.; Chicago; and Seattle. New York State and Massachusetts may well find themselves on the front lines of the plastic bag war this year.

In January, the European Union responded with its first Europe-wide strategy on plastics, which aims to clamp down on single-use plastic items and ensure that they are fully recyclable by 2030.

All of this is part of a growing realization that our feckless use of plastics is out of control. This has become particularly evident in what is happening to the world's oceans. In December, an important milestone was reached when 193 countries signed a United

Nations resolution to monitor plastics disposal in the oceans and 39 countries committed to reducing the quantity of plastics going into the sea.

The United Nations Environment Program estimates that some eight million tons of plastic waste end up in the oceans each year, while a 2016 World Economic Forum report projects that there will be more plastic than fish by weight in the oceans by 2050 if current trends continue. Plastic production and disposal also generates around 400 million tons of carbon dioxide a year globally, more than total annual emissions from Britain.

Millions of whales, birds, seals and turtles die because they mistake plastic bags for food or because they become ensnared in nets, packing bands and other items. Trillions of microplastics end up in the ocean, with seafood eaters ingesting an estimated 11,000 tiny pieces annually. Plastic fibers have also been found in tap water around the world; in one study, researchers found that 94 percent of water samples in the United States were affected. The impact on human health from direct exposure to microplastics is unknown.

One of the most direct ways to begin to address this problem is by taking on the single-use plastic bag.

Following in the footsteps of California, Massachusetts may attempt this year to impose a statewide solution to the plastic bag problem. In December, Boston's mayor, Martin Walsh, signed an ordinance banning single-use plastic bags in city stores. With around 60 other municipalities in the state restricting or imposing fees on these bags, the State Legislature is considering banning them.

New York is another potential battleground. Efforts by former Mayor Michael Bloomberg and by Mayor Bill de Blasio to introduce a bag fee have been stymied in part by opposition from the "big plastic" lobby.

Last year Gov. Andrew Cuomo blocked a law that would have imposed a 5-cent fee on plastic bags in New York City and called instead for a statewide solution. The task force he established identified eight options in a report released in January, including voluntary initiatives, outright bans and fees. But it makes no specific recommendations.

In choosing a solution, it is important to understand the real cause of the plastic bag problem: the myth of free plastic. Retailers pay up to 5 cents per plastic bag, but the cost is hidden, passed on to shoppers through higher grocery prices. This is, no doubt, a brilliant business model for plastic manufacturers, but it has had a devastating impact on the planet.

Fees charged to consumers for each plastic bag undermine the foundation of this myth. They have a long track record of success, and not just across American cities. They have been effective in Denmark, Hong Kong, South Africa, Britain and Botswana. The average Dane, for example, now uses just four single-use plastic bags a year, after the introduction of a fee in 1994.

Some see fees as a regressive tax on seniors, the sick or the poor, but these arguments do not hold water. It is unjust to charge more for staples like food so that discretionary plastic items can be offered free, especially when there are alternatives. In any case, reusable bags can be provided for those in need.

Fees set above 15 cents that flow to an environmental fund strike a good balance between flexibility and effectiveness. They can be more politically acceptable than outright bans. For example, a survey of Irish citizens revealed that a remarkable 91 percent welcomed the fee because they witnessed the drop in litter and found reusable bags more suitable for carrying groceries.

The cultural impact can be game changing. As was the case with smoking indoors, the use of plastic bags becomes less socially acceptable over time once the government moves to restrict them. Reusable bags become the norm quicker than one might imagine, and shoppers seamlessly adapt their daily routines to the new reality. Action aimed at plastic bags can pave the way for further measures to address free coffee cups, lids, stirrers, cutlery, straws and takeout packaging.

When achieved, these small changes to our daily routines can be surprisingly empowering.

JOSEPH CURTIN, a research fellow at the Institute of International and European Affairs, Dublin, and University College Cork, is a member of the Irish government's Climate Change Advisory Council.

Designing the Death of a Plastic

BY XIAOZHI LIM | AUG. 6, 2018

Decades ago, synthetic polymers became popular because they were cheap and durable. Now, scientists are creating material that self-destructs or breaks down for reuse on command.

ADAM FEINBERG had no sooner made a bright yellow thin sheet of plastic than he had to shred it into little pieces. He chose an "I"-shaped mold for the logo of the University of Illinois at Urbana-Champaign where he is a chemist. Then, he filled it with the plastic bits and stuck it in a hot oven.

"I opened up the mold and there was this beautiful yellow 'I'," he recalls. His new plastic passed the first test — it was moldable with heat like regular plastic. But there was another important step left in rethinking the world of durable plastics.

Dr. Feinberg placed the I under a white light, and five minutes later, only half of it remained. The other half had fallen on the ground. Pieced back together, the I had a hole in the middle and in its place was yellow goo.

The plastic did not simply melt. Its building blocks, the synthetic polymers within, had reverted to their molecular units. "It was a phenomenal feeling," he said of the successful experiment.

Most synthetic polymers — Greek for "many parts," because they are long chains of many identical molecules — were not designed to disintegrate or disappear. On the contrary, they were meant to last as long as possible once they began replacing metals and glass in long-lasting things like automobiles and airplanes.

But synthetic polymers became so popular and adaptable that decades later, they're at the root of the global burden of billions of tons of plastic waste. The latest villains in environmental campaigns are disposable plastic products formed from synthetic polymers — straws, cigarette filters, coffee cup lids, etc. Over the past few decades, this

Dr. Feinberg, center, with other researchers, including, from left, Evan Lloyd, Oleg Davydovich, Edgar Mejia and Sydney Butikofer.

mismatch between material and product life span has built up plastic waste in landfills and natural environments, some drifting in oceans until mounds and mounds have reached the ends of the world and bits have been ingested by marine life. Too little gets recycled; in fact some estimates indicate that a mere 10 percent of all plastics are recycled every year.

The European Union has proposed banning single-use plastics, seeking to cut production of items ranging from fishing gear to cotton swabs. Cities in the United States have also been trying to ban some plastics, including grocery bags and those ubiquitous straws that have suddenly turned into the symbol of all that's wrong with our throwaway culture.

The environmental effects of plastic buildup and the declining popularity of plastics have helped to spur chemists on a quest to make new materials with two conflicting requirements: They must be durable,

A plastic sample under U.V. light. The samples contained a yellow dye, DCA, that interacts with the polymer and starts the unzipping process.

but degradable on command. In short, scientists are in search of polymers or plastics with a built-in self-destruct mechanism.

"It's two diametrically opposed criteria that we're trying to juggle," Dr. Feinberg said. It's easier to mold a robust plastic without destroying it, he says, but at the same time, it should not last forever.

"The real trick is to make them stable when you're using them, and unstable when you don't want to use them," says Marc Hillmyer, who leads the Center for Sustainable Polymers at the University of Minnesota.

While not a silver bullet for the problem of plastic waste, self-destructing plastics could also enable new applications in drug delivery, self-healing materials and even some electronics.

The starting point requires picking polymers that are inherently unstable, and often historically overlooked because of their fragility. Given a choice, their units would rather stay as small molecules. What

LYNDON FRENCH FOR THE NEW YORK TIMES

The plastic sample was destroyed after being beamed with high-powered light. Any amount of light will begin to degrade the plastic, but the timescale is inversely proportional to the strength of the light, Dr. Feinberg said.

scientists do is force those molecules to link up into long chains, and then trap the resulting polymers.

Dismantling these polymers is sometimes called unzipping them, because once the polymers encounter a trigger that removes those traps, their units fall off one after another until the polymers have completely switched back to small molecules.

"As soon as you start the process," explains Jeffrey Moore, Dr. Feinberg's supervisor at the University of Illinois, "they just keep going."

Dr. Feinberg's polymers were imprisoned in circular loops instead of being open-ended chains. By themselves, the loops were stable. For the self-destructing plastic, Dr. Feinberg mixed the polymers with a little bit of yellow, light-sensitive dye. When light shines on the plastic, the energized dye molecules rip electrons out from the polymers. The loops break, exposing the polymer ends, and the polymers unzip.

Other scientists trap their polymers by capping the ends of the long chains or linking the chains together into networks. By designing these traps to fail upon meeting certain triggers like light or acid, scientists can control exactly how and when their polymers unzip.

"We can have a big change in properties or complete degradation of the polymer just from one event," says Elizabeth Gillies, a polymer chemist at Western University in London, Ontario. On-demand, rapid disintegration gives unzipping polymers an edge over biodegradable ones, she says, as biodegradation is often slow and difficult to control.

In theory, these next-generation polymers could help mitigate pollution problems associated with plastic products. If the units were collected after unzipping to make new polymers, that would lead to chemical recycling. Most recycling done today simply involves melting the plastic and remolding it.

"In my view it has great potential, the problem is to make it cheap enough and to make the properties competitive enough to be useful and have market penetration for the consumer," Dr. Hillmyer said.

Economically speaking, replacing the most widely used polymers like polyethylene (grocery bags), polypropylene (fishing nets) or polyterephthalate (single-use bottles) with unzipping polymers is not feasible.

"Packaging plastic is the cheapest thing ever," Dr. Gillies said.

Instead, scientists like Dr. Hillmyer are focusing their attention on higher-value materials like the polyurethane foams commonly found in mattresses and car seats. In 2016, Dr. Hillmyer and his team made a polyurethane from unzipping polymers that was chemically recyclable. Molecular units derived from sugar linked up to make the polymers, which then cross-linked into polyurethane networks. The foam remains stable at room temperature but unzips into units if heated above 400 degrees Fahrenheit.

Using chemically recyclable materials could become practical especially if companies begin taking responsibility for their products

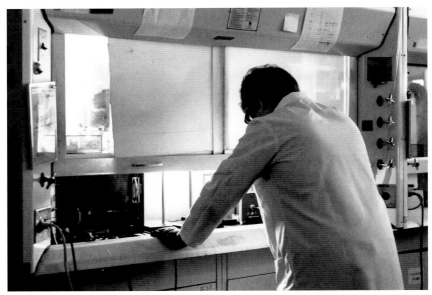

Research by Dr. Feinberg and others is a step toward rethinking plastics and their durability.

after their useful life, Dr. Hillmyer said. He co-founded a start-up company Valerian Materials to commercialize the recyclable polyurethane. If car companies had to take back a used car, for instance, it might make sense to have an internal chemical recycling system to make new materials from old ones, he says.

"It is literally feedstock recovery," says Jeannette Garcia, a polymer chemist at IBM.

Unzipping polymers could also produce adhesives that can be turned off. That would help separate complex objects and materials like toys or Formica surfaces into their individual components for recycling. "We do a terrible job of recycling laminates, composites and even electronics," says Scott Phillips, a polymer chemist at Boise State University.

Dr. Phillips and Hyungwoo Kim, now at Chonnam National University in South Korea, introduced a tiny amount of unzipping polymer into a common, cheap polymer. By themselves, neither polymer is sticky. But when mixed, they cross-link into networks, turning into a sticky, gray goo. To turn the adhesive off, Dr. Phillips and Dr. Kim applied fluoride to the edges of two microscopic glass slides stuck together, and the glass slides fell apart within minutes.

Having unzipping polymers and fully recyclable products is a step forward, but consumers still have to do their recycling right. "Pollution exists because the material wasn't collected," says Steve Alexander who leads the Association of Plastic Recyclers. "If you can't sort properly, no matter what it is, it is just trash." Collection and sorting remain the biggest problems for recyclers today, he says.

The key, says Ramani Narayan, a polymer chemist at Michigan State University, is to have clear, well-defined disposal environments for any object that's reached its end-of-life.

Arguably, he says, biodegradable plastics also have a self-destruct mechanism, provided they end up in the right place with the right microbes. But they've suffered from years of false advertising and consumer confusion. For that, Dr. Narayan is leading a push toward compostable plastics, starting with disposable utensils and food packaging from his spinoff company Natur-Tec. Compost could divert not only single-use plastics associated with food, but also food waste.

"By using the word 'compostable,' it defines the environment," he says, and that, for consumers trying to pick the right bin, is "critical."

Beyond recycling, unzipping polymers can enable new applications ranging from drug delivery to materials that automatically heal themselves, Dr. Moore said.

While self-destructing biomedical implants or electronics are still far-off into the future, scientists like Dr. Gillies are making smart packaging from unzipping polymers. Not to carry groceries, but for payloads like cancer drugs that could be released in tumors or fertilizer only when needed in fields.

For these applications, the units must be safe and benign. A potential candidate is glyoxylate, says Dr. Gillies, which is a molecule that

A sample of the polymer Cyclic poly(phthalaldehyde), or cPPA, powder on a heat plate.

occurs naturally in soil microorganisms. Dr. Gillies' team made unzipping polymers from glyoxylate units and put different caps on them so that they could be deployed in many different scenarios.

"We have a universal backbone and we can just change the end cap to make it responsive to different things," says Dr. Gillies, like light in the fields or a low oxygen environment in tumors.

For Dr. Moore, the goal is to make materials that can heal themselves. "We want our materials to be able to recover from damage and maintain performance over long periods of time," he says.

Dr. Moore envisions filling tiny capsules made from unzipping polymers with healing agents and then embedding the capsules in coatings. Perhaps they respond to light, he says, so that when a cellphone's coating cracks, for example, the light that penetrates will trigger capsule degradation. Those healing agents then spill out to fill the cracks. Then, the coating will automatically be good as new, reducing the need to get a new device.

While waiting for these next-generation polymers to appear, current commercial plastics are still being pumped out on the scale of 400 million metric tons a year. And those plastics were intended to be as strong, as robust and to last as long as possible, says Dr. Garcia.

"Designing new polymers is going to be absolutely important and absolutely necessary," says Dr. Garcia. But a bigger problem, she says, is learning how to break down legacy polymers of plastic waste in a similar way, ideally into their building blocks.

"It's almost like a holy grail challenge."

Giant Trap Is Deployed to Catch Plastic Littering the Pacific Ocean

BY CHRISTINA CARON | SEPT. 9, 2018

A MULTIMILLION-DOLLAR floating boom designed to corral plastic debris littering the Pacific Ocean deployed from San Francisco Bay on Saturday as part of a larger high-stakes and ambitious undertaking.

The 2,000-foot-long unmanned structure was the product of about $20 million in funding from the Ocean Cleanup, a nonprofit that aims to trap up to 150,000 pounds of plastic during the boom's first year at sea. Within five years, with the creation of dozens more booms, the organization hopes to clean half of the Great Pacific Garbage Patch.

The patch, a gyre of trash between California and Hawaii, comprises an estimated 1.8 trillion pieces of scattered detritus, including at least 87,000 tons of plastic.

Over the next several days, the boom will be towed to a site where it will undergo two weeks of testing. If everything goes as planned, the boom will then be brought to the garbage patch, nearly 1,400 miles offshore, where it is expected to arrive by mid-October, said Boyan Slat, 24, the Dutch inventor and entrepreneur who founded Ocean Cleanup.

The cleanup system is supposed to work like this: After the boom detaches from the towing vessel, the current is expected to pull it into the shape of a "U." As it drifts along, propelled by the wind and waves, it should trap plastic "like Pac-Man," the foundation said on its website. The captured plastic would then be transported back to land, sorted and recycled.

The boom has an impenetrable skirt that hangs nearly 10 feet below to catch smaller pieces of plastic. The nonprofit said marine life would be able to pass underneath.

But the ocean can be unpredictable, and simulation models are no guarantee of future performance.

"There's worry that you can't remove the plastic without removing marine life at the same time," said George Leonard, chief scientist at the Ocean Conservancy. "We know from the fishing industry if you put any sort of structure in the open ocean, it acts as a fish-aggregating device."

Small fish, drawn to a new structure, can attract bigger fish, he added, creating an "entire ecological community."

It is unclear how well the boom would fare on the open ocean, where it faces high winds, corrosive salt water and other environmental challenges. And then there's the question of whether it is possible to clean half of the garbage patch in just five years.

"I think the big challenge here is not the long-term goal but the short-term goal," Mr. Leonard said on Saturday. "Can it remove plastic at all?"

Mr. Slat, the chief executive of Ocean Cleanup, shared the same worry in a video posted on Facebook.

"And to me this is where I think my largest anxiety lies at this point in time," he said of the system's ability to collect and retain plastic. "First of all, it's something that we haven't really been able to test very well."

But on Saturday morning, Mr. Slat was decidedly optimistic.

"I've definitely never been so confident about the chance of success as I am today," he said.

Since the start of Ocean Cleanup in 2013, donors have contributed nearly $35 million, Mr. Slat said. Much of that money paid for the boom and helped underwrite research like a study published in the journal Scientific Reports, which quantified the full extent of the garbage patch. Future booms are estimated to cost about $5.8 million each.

Major sponsors include Marc Benioff, the chief executive of Salesforce.com, and Peter Thiel, the co-founder of PayPal.

Skeptics questioned whether this was the most economically efficient way to address the problem.

"I fully agree that this is not the full solution to plastic pollution," Mr. Slat said.

While it's necessary to prevent more plastic from entering the ocean, what is there already isn't going to go away by itself, he added.

"We have to clean it up at some point in time and, actually, I would say the sooner the better," he said.

9 Ways to Cut Down on Plastic

BY STEVEN KURUTZ | FEB. 16, 2019

It's all about reducing single-use plastics.

DROWNING IN PLASTIC, but not sure how to set yourself free? Plastic purgers say you can drastically reduce, if not eliminate, your plastic consumption by changing a few daily habits. Here are nine steps to get you started.

1. Carry a reusable bag.

This is Plastic-Free-Living 101. Take a cloth bag to the grocery store, farmers' market, drugstore and anywhere else you may be given a plastic bag.

ADAM AMENGUAL FOR THE NEW YORK TIMES

Going plastic free means wooden toothbrushes and D.I.Y. toothpaste.

2. Use plastic-free containers.

Glass or metal jars can be used to store grains, nuts, flour and other foods, as well as laundry detergent, dish soap and body creams. But don't automatically purge all of your plastic containers; that creates unnecessary waste.

3. Pack a travel kit.

Bamboo cutlery and a nonplastic food tray, straw and water bottle will eliminate the need for most single-use plastics while on-the-go. "Restaurants and vendors all over the world are getting much more used to people bringing their own containers," said Jay Sinha, a founder of Life Without Plastic, an online store.

4. Buy in bulk.

To avoid food packaging, shop the bulk aisle at the market and bring your own glass containers. Weigh the jar beforehand to avoid being overcharged.

5. Buy used items.

Some household plastic is unavoidable, especially in modern appliances. So until they make an all-metal vacuum cleaner, Beth Terry, who writes the blog My Plastic-free Life, suggests buying secondhand, through Craigslist or at a thrift shop. "I'm not buying new plastic," she said. "I'm also avoiding the packaging."

6. Recycle "good" plastics.

Clear plastic bottles, bottles for shampoos, yogurt containers, toys and reusable food containers have a higher probability of being recycled. Disposable cutlery, cling wrap and coffee cups and lids have very low probability.

7. Wear natural clothes.

Synthetic fibers from clothing "are an enormous plastic pollution problem," said Mr. Sinha, because they are a key contributor to microplastic pollution. Choose clothing made of fabrics like cotton, wool, hemp and silk.

8. Make your own.

With so many toiletries packaged in plastic, Chantal Plamondon, a founder of Life Without Plastic, became a home chemist. "We make our own toothpaste out of baking soda, coconut oil and essential oils," she said. "We make body creams out of coconut or macadamia oil."

9. Do without.

If it's plastic or nothing, you can always choose nothing.

STEVEN KURUTZ joined The Times in 2011 and wrote for the City and Home sections before joining Style. He was previously a reporter at The Wall Street Journal and Details.

Plastic Bags, or Paper? Here's What to Consider When You Hit the Grocery Store

BY BRAD PLUMER | MARCH 29, 2019

WASHINGTON — The decision by New York State to ban single-use plastic bags from retail stores makes it a good time to revisit everyone's favorite environmental quandary: paper or plastic?

Unfortunately, there's not a simple answer on whether paper or plastic bags are better for the environment. They both have downsides, but there are a few broad lessons to keep in mind when you're hitting the grocery store.

Plastic bags, which often take centuries to decompose, can create a dreadful waste problem even though they're far from the largest source of plastic waste in America — about 12 percent of the total.

On the other hand, paper bags typically require more energy and greenhouse gas emissions to produce, which isn't great from a global warming standpoint.

Reusable bags can be a decent compromise, provided you hold onto them and use them often. Ultimately, though, what you put inside the bag, particularly your food choices, will most likely matter a lot more for the environment than what type of bag you use.

THE TROUBLE WITH PLASTIC BAGS: LITTER

American shoppers use more than 100 billion lightweight polyethylene plastic bags each year, and only a small portion are ever recycled. Most recycling centers can't deal with them — they just clog up the machinery — and so the majority of plastic bags end up in landfills, where they can take up to 1,000 years to degrade.

To be fair, a plastic bag doesn't cause too much harm sitting in a landfill. The bigger problem arises when people don't dispose of their

Plastic bags are only a fraction of America's overall plastic trash, but they've become a highly visible sign of waste.

bags properly, and the plastic ends up fluttering around in the wild, clogging up waterways and threatening wildlife.

San Jose, Calif., for instance, found that plastic bags made up about 12 percent of the litter in its creeks before implementing a local bag ban in 2012. And, just last week, a dead sperm whale washed ashore in Indonesia with two dozen plastic bags in its gut, along with other trash.

So, even though plastic bags are only a small fraction of America's overall plastic trash, they've become a highly visible sign of waste.

THE TROUBLE WITH PAPER BAGS: CARBON EMISSIONS

So does that mean paper bags, which degrade more easily, are a better option? Not necessarily. Climate change has become the biggest environmental issue of our time, so it's worth looking at things from an emissions standpoint. And on that score, paper bags fare worse.

Even though paper bags are made from trees, which are, in theory, a renewable resource, it takes significantly more energy to create pulp and manufacture a paper bag than it does to make a single-use plastic bag from oil.

Back in 2011, Britain's Environment Agency conducted a life-cycle assessment of various bag options, looking at every step of the production process. The conclusion? You'd have to reuse a paper bag at least three times before its environmental impact equaled that of a high-density polyethylene plastic bag used only once. And if plastic bags were reused repeatedly, they looked even better.

Paper bags can more easily be recycled or even composted, but the British study found that even these actions didn't make a huge difference in the broader analysis. Unless you're reusing your paper bags a lot, they look like a poorer option from a global warming standpoint.

REUSABLE BAGS ARE A DECENT OPTION — IF YOU ACTUALLY REUSE THEM

That same British analysis also looked into reusable options, like heavier, more durable plastic bags or cotton bags. And it found that these are only sustainable options if you use them very frequently.

Making a cotton shopping bag is hardly cost-free. Growing cotton requires a fair bit of energy, land, fertilizer and pesticides, which can have all sorts of environmental effects — from greenhouse gas emissions to nitrogen pollution in waterways.

The study found that an avid shopper would have to reuse his or her cotton bag 131 times before it had a smaller global warming impact than a lightweight plastic bag used only once. And, depending on the make, more durable plastic bags would have to be used at least 4 to 11 times before they made up for their heftier upfront climate costs.

So if you're going to opt for a reusable bag for environmental reasons, make sure you actually reuse it — often.

WHAT'S IN THE BAG MOST LIKELY MATTERS MORE THAN THE BAG ITSELF

It never hurts to think about bag choices. But keep in mind that if you're going to the grocery store, the food you purchase and place in that bag probably has a vastly bigger effect on the environment than whatever you use to haul it home.

Our global food system, after all, is responsible for one-quarter of humanity's planet-warming greenhouse gas emissions — with meat and dairy having a disproportionately large impact. By contrast, packaging makes up only about 5 percent of the food system's footprint. Compared with, say, the effects of clearing away vast swaths of forest to grow feed or raise livestock, our bags are a much smaller deal.

Put another way, a pound of beef bought at the supermarket will have roughly 25 times the global warming impact as the disposable plastic bag it's carried in. So if you're looking for ways to slim down your personal carbon footprint, taking a closer look at your dietary choices isn't a bad place to start.

BRAD PLUMER is a reporter covering climate change, energy policy and other environmental issues for The Times's climate team.

Tackling the Plastic Problem,
One City (or Country) at a Time

BY ZACH WICHTER | APRIL 22, 2019

PLASTIC IS PRACTICALLY an invasive species.

It's clogging the oceans, littering cities and tainting wilderness areas that are supposed to be pristine.

Single-use plastic items — everything from disposable water bottles to shopping bags handed out like grocery-store door prizes — are among the most invasive forms of plastic. Single-use plastics are inarguably convenient, but those forks from on-the-go meals have to wind up somewhere, and very often, they become litter.

There is no comprehensive global plan to stop their spread.

But places around the world are moving to ban some forms of single-use plastics. Rwanda banned plastic bags in 2008. Washington, D.C., has for years charged 5 cents for plastic bags, and earlier this year banned plastic straws and drink stirrers. Other countries and cities are working on or have enacted their own policies. In some areas, tourism-related businesses are leading the charge.

Here are a few different plans of action that tourist-friendly destinations have for tackling their plastic pollution:

BARBADOS

Earlier this month, Barbados enacted a nationwide ban on single-use plastics. It includes food service items from cutlery to Styrofoam containers, and, beginning in January, will be expanded to prohibit plastic shopping bags.

"There will be an immediate sense that Barbados is much tidier and a cleaner location," said Connie Smith, a trustee of the Waste 0 Resources Trust in Barbados, a group that advocates for reducing plastic use.

A beach in Barbados.

The goal, according to officials from the country, is to make Barbados more sustainable and protect the island's biggest tourist draw — its natural landscape. Tourism, after all, is a major component of the economy in Barbados.

"Irrespective of whether you're a local or a visitor, everyone is looking to make more responsible choices," said Petra Roach, the U.S. director of Barbados Tourism Marketing. "We need to be extremely protective of the space that we have."

The officials from Barbados said most businesses and residents supported the new policy, and that educating visitors was fairly easy because many tourists who come to the island live in places that already have some form of their own plastic bans.

Many businesses there offer or will offer biodegradable or compostable alternatives to plastic food service items, but visitors are also encouraged to bring their own containers, like reusable coffee mugs.

"The reality is that we are on a movement toward greater sustainability," Ms. Smith said.

SEATTLE

The West Coast is often seen as an incubator for progressive environmental policies, and Seattle is among the locales leading the charge on reducing plastic waste.

In 2012, the city enacted a ban on plastic bags, and earlier this year started enforcing a long-planned ban on plastic food service items. So far, according to city tourism officials and business leaders, the policies have gotten little pushback.

"It's been accepted broadly and widely as the right thing to do," said Tom Norwalk, president and chief executive of Visit Seattle. "It's something people have come to expect when they visit Seattle and the Northwest, that we have an extreme sensitivity to sustainability."

Overall, he said, locals largely support the policies, and many visitors to the city are environmentally conscious. Even those that aren't generally respect the plastic regulations. Business owners, too, said the bans don't cause too much friction, and in some cases present teaching opportunities about environmental issues.

"When people see it, they're curious about what we're doing," said Bob Donegan, president of Ivar's Restaurants, a chain of more than 20 restaurants around Washington state, with five restaurants in Seattle. The cutlery and plates used in the restaurants are now compostable, and the drinking straws biodegradable. He explained that at the chain's counter-service locations, guests have to sort their own garbage into appropriate bins — trash, recycling and compost. During the height of the summer tourist season, his busiest restaurants assign staffers to help unfamiliar diners throw things away properly.

SCOTLAND

In 2014, Scotland instituted a 5 pence charge for plastic shopping bags.

Although they're not banned outright, the country saw an 80 percent reduction in plastic bag use in the fee's first year.

As a result, there's less plastic litter spread around Scotland's famed wilderness.

"It's very important that we protect it and maintain it for its own sake but also for the tourism," said Janie Neumann, Visit Scotland's industry development manager for sustainability. She added that educating people about ways to reduce their waste and protect the environment makes them more motivated to do so. "Consumer awareness in a way is driving change."

Scotland, along with the larger British and European Union governments, is considering legislation to introduce more stringent plastic policies, including laws that would ban straws or plastic food packaging.

CAMBODIA

In Cambodia, a country that uses about 4.6 million plastic water bottles per month, the manager of a boutique hotel wanted to effect change on his own.

Christian De Boer, the managing director of Jaya House River Park in Siem Reap, started a mission to reduce plastic water bottle waste in 2017. The Refill Not Landfill campaign is a voluntary program for hotels and restaurants to offer their guests reusable water bottles and make free filling stations accessible to participants. The bottles feature a square-shaped QR code that thirsty users can scan to find the nearest refill site.

The campaign is expanding across Southeast Asia and Oceania, and Mr. De Boer said he hopes it can be a model for plastic reduction worldwide, especially in places where clean drinking water is already available at the tap.

"We all know that we need to reduce, we all know that we need to make bigger efforts." Mr. De Boer said. Guests in his hotel are usually excited by the program and he hasn't had anyone ask for a plastic water bottle since it started. "I honestly think the world is ready for this.

Would You Drink Water Out of a Can? Pepsi Wants to Find Out

BY DAVID YAFFE-BELLANY | JUNE 27, 2019

Consumers have already adjusted to, or even welcomed, cans for seltzer, craft beer and even wine. Will they feel the same way about still water?

ABOUT THE LAST THING Selena James wants to do is drink water from a can.

"Something like that would scare me," Ms. James, 53, said after buying a bottle of Mountain Dew at a corner deli in Brooklyn. "You see juice in a can, not water. You see water in a bottle."

Her instinctual aversion to water in a can highlights a challenge facing one of the world's biggest beverage companies, PepsiCo, as it seeks to persuade consumers to embrace a new product it says is meant to help the environment.

Pepsi said Thursday that starting early next year, its Aquafina brand of water would be test-marketed in aluminum cans at some retailers and food-service providers.

Stacy Taffet, the Pepsi vice president who oversees the company's water brands, acknowledged that while many kinds of fizzy water already came in aluminum containers, drinking still water from a can would be "a newer behavior" for many people.

"Our goal is to be a little bit ahead of consumers here," she said, "and help nudge them in the right direction."

Consumers are also nudging Pepsi. In recent years, public sentiment has turned against single-use plastic items, which can end up accumulating in landfills or floating in oceans. Across the world, only 9 percent of all the plastic ever made has been recycled; by contrast, 67 percent of the aluminum bought by consumers every year is reused.

And consumers have already adjusted to, or even welcomed, cans for seltzer, craft beer and even wine. Pepsi also plans to sell its carbonated water, Bubly, in cans and to put Lifewtr, a purified water that contains electrolytes, in bottles made entirely from recycled plastic.

But there's a limit to how much environmental good Pepsi's new packaging can achieve. While putting water in aluminum cans and recycled plastic is a step forward for the industry, the best way for consumers to protect the environment would be to give up packaged water entirely, said Peter Gleick, the author of a book about bottled water.

Pepsi is "trying to do better at things that maybe we shouldn't be doing at all," Mr. Gleick said.

Many of the details of Pepsi's canned water experiment remain unclear. Ms. Taffet said the company was still working out where the water would be sold and what the price would be.

In the meantime, consumers who want an environmentally friendly alternative to plastic bottles have other options. In recent years, Boxed Water, a Michigan company that packages its water in paper containers resembling milk cartons, has gained something of a cult following.

And a new brand, Ever & Ever, packages water in bottle-shaped aluminum cans with screw tops.

Despite growing public awareness of the environmental consequences, sales of bottled water have continued to increase in the United States in recent years, rising more than 5 percent in 2018, according to the Beverage Marketing Corporation. That growth has helped offset a decline in the core soda business of companies like Pepsi and Coca-Cola.

"Consumers are clearly interested in the convenience of bottled water, the affordability," said Duane Stanford, the executive editor of the trade publication Beverage Digest. He described Pepsi's packaging move as a low-risk experiment that would not send the company "too far down the road too quickly toward a decision that might not be the best when it comes to how consumers react."

The kind of skepticism that Pepsi may face was on full display in the bottled-water aisle at a Target at the Atlantic Terminal Mall in Brooklyn.

Hector Orantes, who was in the store, said he periodically stocked up on bottles of Poland Spring water at a BJ's Wholesale Club. Mr. Orantes, a gym teacher from Queens, said that something about the idea of drinking water from an aluminum can felt strange to him. He said he preferred that his water receptacles be transparent.

"I need to see the contents of the water," he said. "I need to see there's nothing inside."

Less Trash, More Schools —
One Plastic Brick at a Time

BY ANEMONA HARTOCOLLIS | JULY 27, 2019

Plastic garbage collected by a women's group is being recycled into bricks and used to build schools in West Africa.

ABIDJAN, IVORY COAST — She left home before dawn. Her four children were still asleep in her cement block house in Abobo, a maze of shops and houses occupied by dockworkers, taxi drivers, factory laborers and street sellers.

She and a friend crossed into the upscale neighborhood of Angré, home to doctors and businessmen. They tossed the plastic castoffs of the consumer class into bags slung over their shoulders as the cocks crowed and the sun peeked over villa walls draped with bougainvillea.

Mariam Coulibaly is part of a legion of women in Abidjan who make their living picking up plastic waste on the city streets and selling it for recycling. Now they are lead players in a project that turns trash into plastic bricks to build schools across the country.

They are working with a Colombian company to convert plastic waste — a scourge of modern life — into an asset that will help women earn a decent living while cleaning up the environment and improving education.

She sees it as a chance to better her life, maybe even to rise into the middle class.

"We don't get good prices" from the current buyers, Ms. Coulibaly said. "This will help us."

In the past year, the venture has built nine demonstration classrooms out of recycled plastic bricks in Gonzagueville, a scrappy neighborhood on the outskirts of Abidjan, and in two small farming villages, Sakassou and Divo. The first schools were built with bricks imported from Colombia. But in the fall, a factory now rising in an Abidjan industrial park will begin making the bricks locally.

Students and residents gathered by plastic bricks outside their school in the Sakassou village.

The new plastic-brick classrooms are badly needed. Some classrooms now pack in 90 students, according to the country's education minister. The company building the factory, Conceptos Plásticos, has a contract with UNICEF to deliver 528 classrooms for about 26,400 students, at 50 students per classroom.

In the tiny village of Sakassou, people draw water from the well with a foot pump, raise pigs and chickens, and cook over open fires. Until this year, the children went to school in a traditional mud-brick and wood building. The mud brick eroded in the sun and rain and had to be constantly repaired.

But the three new plastic classrooms could last practically forever. The interlocking bricks look like black and gray Legos. They are fire retardant and stay cool in hot weather. The other day, villagers used one of the brightly decorated classrooms to hold a village meeting.

"This is ten times better," said Joachim Koffi Konan, the school director in Sakassou.

The project would be impossible without the organizing skills of Ms. Coulibaly, president of a 200-strong women's community association called "The Fighting Women."

She has been collecting trash for about twenty years, since she was 15. Her husband drives a woro-woro, a shared taxi.

After collecting trash the other morning, she went home to do the housework, then returned to work at night, this time in the vast open-air market of Adjamé at closing time.

She and other women waltzed through dimly lit alleyways, past the fishmonger and the tailor still bent over his sewing machine. They even picked up the small bags of plastic used to sell a quick gulp of water on the street.

While the women wait for the factory to open, they sell their plastic to middlemen — most are men — at a recycling market in Abobo-Baoulé.

On a recent Saturday, one of the buyers, a former yam pushcart vendor named Sidibé Moussa, weighed each woman's plastic harvest by hanging it from a hand-held bronze scale. He resells the plastic to a factory that recycles it into chairs, sandals and basins. Bottles are often washed, filled with juice and resold on the street.

At the recycling market, the women multitasked, drying attiéké, a manioc couscous, on plastic tarps spread on the ground among the palm trees and the mesh bags of plastic waste. Women and children crushed aluminum cans by hand, pounding them with the same type of large wooden pestles used to make foufou, a staple made of plantains and cassava.

The country's official minimum wage is roughly $25 per week, though many people earn far less. The women say they earn $8.50 to $17 a week.

Ms. Coulibaly puts her money into private school tuition for her three school-age children, who tell her they want to become a pilot, a doctor and a police officer.

A member of the Abobo women's association sorts through plastics, which she intends to save until after the factory opens so she can sell it for the higher profit that the factory has promised.

The women in the association each contribute some money to a fund which is then redistributed, ensuring that even a woman who is sick will receive some income.

When they start selling to the factory, they may be able to double or triple their income, the company says. That's because the factory will buy types of plastic, like snack packaging and cellphone parts, that the women cannot sell now.

Some of Ms. Coulibaly's neighbors have suggested that she and the other women will be exploited. But she said she is confident that the project will deliver the higher pay, equipment and sacks that have been promised.

The project has the blessing of Kandia Camara, Ivory Coast's outspoken education minister, who says it can only lift women up.

"For us, it's not a humiliating profession," Ms. Camara said in an interview at her office, decorated with photographs of her with other prominent women, like Ivanka Trump and Christine Lagarde, the former chairman of the International Monetary Fund. "It is a job organized for them, their financial autonomy, their dignity, family, society, and their contribution to the development of the country."

The project was the brainchild of Aboubacar Kampo, a medical doctor, who just ended a term as Ivory Coast representative for UNICEF. He recruited Conceptos Plásticos, a for-profit plastic recycling company with a social mission of building housing and creating jobs for poor people. The founders of the company, Oscar Andrés Méndez and his wife, Isabel Cristina Gámez, agreed to work with Dr. Kampo after visiting Ivory Coast last year.

They were moved by the sight of women, carrying babies, picking up trash in Akouedo, a landfill notorious as a dumping site for hazardous waste, and thought they could help. "It had a big impact for us," Mr. Méndez said.

The couple moved to Abidjan in June to get the project up and running, and they are planning to expand into other parts of West Africa.

They expect to employ 30 people at the factory and to buy plastic from about 1,000 women in its first year of operation.

The first few classrooms cost about $14,500 each, compared to $16,500 for a cement classroom, said Mr. Méndez. He expects the price to drop about 20 percent when the bricks are made locally.

There is no shortage of plastic waste. Abidjan produces about 300 tons of it a day, but only 5 percent of it is recycled, the project organizers say. Each classroom takes about five tons of plastic trash to build.

Dr. Kampo envisions expanding to plastic housing for teachers and latrines for schools. The teachers in Sakassou share houses while their families are housed in other villages. In Gonzagueville, there are 14 latrines for 2,700 children and their teachers.

Before all this happened, the leader of the Fighting Women had been considering a new line of work: selling cold drinks.

But now, Ms. Coulibaly says, "We think there is a future in plastic."

LOUCOUMANE COULIBALY contributed reporting from Abidjan, Ivory Coast.

Glossary

biodegradable Capable of being decomposed by living organisms.

climate change The long-term alteration in global climate patterns due to increased levels of greenhouse gases in the Earth's atmosphere.

disposable Designed to be used briefly and thrown away.

ecology The study of the relationship between organisms and their environment.

hydrocarbon An organic compound consisting of hydrogen and carbon; a chief component of petroleum and natural gas.

petrochemical Substances derived from petroleum and natural gas that are integral in the manufacture of plastics products.

plastic A synthetic compound derived from petrochemicals that is malleable and versatile, but its chemical structure makes it slow to decompose.

polymer A substance composed of long chains of repeating molecules.

polystyrene A synthetic resin; one of the most widely used forms of plastic.

rate of decomposition The speed at which matter is broken down into simpler components.

recycling The method of converting waste into reusable material, thereby reducing pollution and energy usage.

synthetic Artificial; produced by chemical synthesis to imitate natural material.

Media Literacy Terms

"Media literacy" refers to the ability to access, understand, critically assess and create media. The following terms are important components of media literacy, and they will help you critically engage with the articles in this title.

angle The aspect of a news story that a journalist focuses on and develops.

attribution The method by which a source is identified or by which facts and information are assigned to the person who provided them.

balance Principle of journalism that both perspectives of an argument should be presented in a fair way.

bias A disposition of prejudice in favor of a certain idea, person or perspective.

commentary A type of story that is an expression of opinion on recent events by a journalist generally known as a commentator.

credibility The quality of being trustworthy and believable, said of a journalistic source.

critical review A type of story that describes an event or work of art, such as a theater performance, film, concert, book, restaurant, radio or television program, exhibition or musical piece, and offers critical assessment of its quality and reception.

editorial Article of opinion or interpretation.

feature story Article designed to entertain as well as to inform.

human interest story A type of story that focuses on individuals and how events or issues affect their life, generally offering a sense of relatability to the reader.

impartiality Principle of journalism that a story should not reflect a journalist's bias and should contain balance.

intention The motive or reason behind something, such as the publication of a news story.

interview story A type of story in which the facts are gathered primarily by interviewing another person or persons.

motive The reason behind something, such as the publication of a news story or a source's perspective on an issue.

news story An article or style of expository writing that reports news, generally in a straightforward fashion and without editorial comment.

op-ed An opinion piece that reflects a prominent individual's opinion on a topic of interest.

paraphrase The summary of an individual's words, with attribution, rather than a direct quotation of their exact words.

quotation The use of an individual's exact words indicated by the use of quotation marks and proper attribution.

reliability The quality of being dependable and accurate, said of a journalistic source.

rhetorical device Technique in writing intending to persuade the reader or communicate a message from a certain perspective.

source The origin of the information reported in journalism.

style A distinctive use of language in writing or speech; also a news or publishing organization's rules for consistent use of language with regard to spelling, punctuation, typography and capitalization, usually regimented by a house style guide.

tone A manner of expression in writing or speech.

Media Literacy Questions

1. What type of story is "No Road Back to Natural Materials" (on page 19)? Can you identify another article in this collection that is the same type of story? What elements helped you come to your conclusion?

2. Does Barry Commoner demonstrate the journalistic principle of impartiality in his article "The Promise and Perils of Petrochemicals" (on page 22)? If so, how did he do so? If not, what could Commoner have included to make the article more impartial?

3. Does "Leaders of Plastics Industry Seeking 25% Recycling Goal" (on page 96) use multiple sources? What are the strengths of using multiple sources in a journalistic piece? What are the weaknesses of relying heavily on only one or a few sources?

4. Compare the headlines of "Plastic Panic" (on page 108) and "Before You Flush Your Contact Lenses, You Might Want to Know This" (on page 116). Which is a more compelling headline, and why? How could the less compelling headline be changed to better draw the reader's interest?

5. "Just a Few Pieces of Plastic Can Kill Sea Turtles" (on page 118) features a photograph. What does this photograph add to the article?

6. In "Microplastics Find Their Way Into Your Gut, a Pilot Study Finds" (on page 122), Douglas Quenqua paraphrases information from a scientific study. What are the strengths of the use of a paraphrase as opposed to a direct quote? What are the weaknesses?

7. Analyze the authors' reporting in "Whale's Death in Thailand Points to Global Scourge: Plastic in Oceans" (on page 113) and "Whale Is Found Dead in Italy With 48 Pounds of Plastic in Its Stomach" (on page 130). Do you think one journalist is more balanced in their reporting than the other? If so, why do you think so?

8. Identify each of the sources in "Raising Awareness of Plastic Waste" (on page 167) as a primary source or a secondary source. Evaluate the reliability and credibility of each source. How does your evaluation of each source change your perspective on this article?

9. The article "Let's Bag Plastic Bags" (on page 176) is an example of an op-ed. Identify how Joseph Curtin's attitude and tone help convey his opinion on the topic.

10. What is the intention of the article "9 Ways to Cut Down on Plastic" (on page 193)? How effectively does it achieve its intended purpose?

11. Identify the various sources cited in the article "Tackling the Plastic Problem, One City (or Country) at a Time" (on page 200). How does Zach Wichter attribute information to each of these sources in his article? How effective are Wichter's attributions in helping the reader identify his sources?

Citations

All citations in this list are formatted according to the Modern Language Association's (MLA) style guide.

BOOK CITATION

THE NEW YORK TIMES EDITORIAL STAFF. *Plastic: Can the Damage Be Repaired?* New York: New York Times Educational Publishing, 2020.

ONLINE ARTICLE CITATIONS

ALBECK-RIPKA, LIVIA. "The 'Great Pacific Garbage Patch' Is Ballooning, 87,000 Tons of Plastic and Counting." *The New York Times*, 22 Mar. 2018, https://www.nytimes.com/2018/03/22/climate/great-pacific-garbage-patch.html.

BROWNE, MALCOLM W. "Synthetics Go to New Lengths in Outperforming Natural Materials." *The New York Times*, 31 Mar. 1981, https://www.nytimes.com/1981/03/31/science/synthetics-go-to-new-lengths-in-outperforming-natural-materials.html.

CARON, CHRISTINA. "Giant Trap Is Deployed to Catch Plastic Littering the Pacific Ocean." *The New York Times*, 9 Sept. 2019, https://www.nytimes.com/2018/09/09/science/ocean-cleanup-great-pacific-garbage-patch.html.

CHAVEZ, LYDIA. "Plastics: Fast Growth Stalls." *The New York Times*, 5 Feb. 1982, https://www.nytimes.com/1982/02/05/business/plastics-fast-growth-stalls.html.

COMMONER, BARRY. "The Promise and Perils of Petrochemicals." *The New York Times*, 25 Sept. 1977, https:www.nytimes.com/1977/09/25/archives/the-promise-and-perils-of-the-petrochemicals-industry.html.

CORKERY, MICHAEL. "Beverage Companies Embrace Recycling, Until It Costs Them." *The New York Times*, 4 July 2019, https://www.nytimes.com/2019/07/04/business/plastic-recycling-bottle-bills.html.

CORKERY, MICHAEL. "A Giant Factory Rises to Make a Product Filling Up

the World: Plastic." 12 Aug. 2019, https://www.nytimes.com/2019/08/12
/business/energy-environment/plastics-shell-pennsylvania-plant.html.

CURTIN, JOSEPH. "Let's Bag Plastic Bags." *The New York Times*, 3 Mar. 2018,
https://www.nytimes.com/2018/03/03/opinion/sunday/plastic-bags
-pollution-oceans.html.

FEDER, BARNABY J. "Pepsi and Coke to Offer Recycled-Plastic Bottles." *The
New York Times*, 5 Dec. 1990, https://www.nytimes.com/1990/12/05
/business/pepsi-and-coke-to-offer-recycled-plastic-bottles.html.

FISHMAN, JOANNE A. "A Closer Look At Ocean Pollution." *The New York Times*,
22 Apr. 1979, https://www.nytimes.com/1979/04/22/archives/long-island
-weekly-a-closer-look-at-ocean-pollution-a-closer-look-a.html.

GLUSAC, ELAINE. "Are Mini Shampoo Bottles the New Plastic Straw?" *The
New York Times*, 29 July 2019, https://www.nytimes.com/2019/07/29
/travel/plastic-straws-mini-shampoo-bottles.html.

GREENWOOD, VERONIQUE. "Before You Flush Your Contact Lenses, You Might
Want to Know This." *The New York Times*, 19 Aug. 2018, https://www
.nytimes.com/2018/08/19/science/contact-lenses-pollution.html.

GOLD, ALLAN R. "In Its Latest Recycling Effort, Staten Island Targets Plastic."
The New York Times, 11 Sept. 1990, https://www.nytimes.com/1990/09/11
/nyregion/in-its-latest-recycling-effort-si-targets-plastic.html.

HAITCH, RICHARD. "The Environment Versus Plastic." *The New York Times*,
28 Dec. 1986, https://www.nytimes.com/1986/12/28/us/follow-up-on-the
-news-the-environment-versus-plastic.html.

HANLEY, ROBERT. "A Second Life for Plastic Cups? Science Turns Them
Into Lumber." *The New York Times*, 22 Feb. 1989, https://www.nytimes
.com/1989/02/22/nyregion/a-second-life-for-plastic-cups-science-turns
-them-into-lumber.html.

HARTOCOLLIS, ANEMONA. "Less Trash, More Schools — One Plastic Brick at
a Time." *The New York Times*, 27 July 2019, https://www.nytimes.com
/2019/07/27/world/africa/recycled-plastic-school-building-conceptos
-plasticos.html.

HINDS, MICHAEL DECOURCY. "Plastic Compound May Be Reviewed." *The
New York Times*, 15 Sept. 1983, https://www.nytimes.com/1983/09/15/us
/plastic-compound-may-be-reviewed.html.

HOLUSHA, JOHN. "Doubts Are Voiced on 'Degradable' Plastic Waste." *The New
York Times*, 25 Oct. 1989, https://www.nytimes.com/1989/10/25/business
/business-technology-doubts-are-voiced-on-degradable-plastic-waste.html.

HOLUSHA, JOHN. "Leaders of Plastics Industry Seeking 25% Recycling Goal." *The New York Times*, 29 Mar. 1991, https://www.nytimes.com/1991/03/29 /business/leaders-of-plastics-industry-seeking-25-recycling-goal.html.

HOLUSHA, JOHN. "Separating Plastic Wheat and Chaff." *The New York Times*, 2 June 1991, https://www.nytimes.com/1991/06/02/business/technology -separating-plastic-wheat-and-chaff.html.

HOLUSHA, JOHN. "A Setback for Polystyrene." *The New York Times*, 18 Nov. 1990, https://www.nytimes.com/1990/11/18/business/a-setback-for -polystyrene.html.

HOLUSHA, JOHN. "Turning Waste Plastics Into Fuels." *The New York Times*, 28 Aug. 1991, https://www.nytimes.com/1991/08/28/business/business -technology-turning-waste-plastics-into-fuels.html.

IVES, MIKE. "Recyclers Cringe as Southeast Asia Says It's Sick of the West's Trash." *The New York Times*, 7 June 2019, https://www.nytimes.com/2019 /06/07/world/asia/asia-trash.html.

IVES, MIKE. "Whale's Death in Thailand Points to Global Scourge: Plastic in Oceans." *The New York Times*, 4 June 2018, https://www.nytimes .com/2018/06/04/world/asia/thailand-whale-plastics-pollution.html.

KERN, LAUREN. "Plastic Panic." *The New York Times*, 9 Mar. 2011, https:// 6thfloor.blogs.nytimes.com/2011/03/09/plastic-panic/.

KERR, PETER. "Debate on Safety of Urea Foam and Plastic Tubing." *The New York Times*, 25 Feb. 1982, https://www.nytimes.com/1982/02/25/garden /debate-on-safety-of-urea-foam-and-plastic-tubing.html.

KLOCKENBRINK, MYRA. "Plastics Industry, Under Pressure, Begins to Invest in Recycling." *The New York Times,* 30 Aug. 1988, https://www.nytimes .com/1988/08/30/science/plastics-industry-under-pressure-begins-to -invest-in-recycling.html.

KOLBERT, ELIZABETH. "Recycling Worries on Plastic Bottles." *The New York Times*, 7 Aug. 1986, https://www.nytimes.com/1986/08/07/garden /recycling-worries-on-plastic-bottles.html.

KURUTZ, STEVEN. "9 Ways to Cut Down on Plastic." *The New York Times*, 16 Feb. 2019, https://www.nytimes.com/2019/02/16/style/plastic-how-to -use-less.html.

LIM, XIAOZHI. "Designing the Death of a Plastic." *The New York Times*, 6 Aug. 2018, https://www.nytimes.com/2018/08/06/science/plastics -polymers-pollution.html.

LYONS, RICHARD D. "Rise in Chemicals Is Causing Alarm." *The New York

Times, 26 Sept. 1971, https://www.nytimes.com/1971/09/26/archives
/rise-in-chemicals-is-causing-alarm-11-in-house-propose-testing-of.html.

MAGRA, ILIANA. "Whale Is Found Dead in Italy With 48 Pounds of Plastic
in Its Stomach." *The New York Times*, 2 Apr. 2019, https://www.nytimes
.com/2019/04/02/world/europe/plastic-whale-dead-italy.html.

NAGOURNEY, ERIC. "Ocean Cleanup Plastic Collector Heading Home. In
Pieces." *The New York Times*, 3 Jan. 2019, https://www.nytimes.com/2019
/01/03/world/americas/great-pacific-garbage-patch-cleanup.html.

THE NEW YORK TIMES. "Huge Role Played by Plastics in War." *The New York
Times*, 3 Jan. 1943, https://www.nytimes.com/1943/01/03/archives/huge
-role-played-by-plastics-in-war-industry-boosted-42-output.html.

THE NEW YORK TIMES. "New Process Cuts Costs of Plastics." *The New York
Times*, 7 Dec. 1943, https://www.nytimes.com/1943/12/07/archives/new
-process-cuts-costs-of-plastics-method-announced-at-chemical.html.

THE NEW YORK TIMES. "Plastics Gains Forecast." *The New York Times*,
26 May 1943, https://www.nytimes.com/1943/05/26/archives/plastics
-gains-forecast-dr-wendt-sees-new-industries-in-the-postwar.html.

PLUMER, BRAD. "Plastic Bags, or Paper? Here's What to Consider When You
Hit the Grocery Store." *The New York Times*, 29 Mar. 2019, https://www
.nytimes.com/2019/03/29/climate/plastic-paper-shopping-bags.html.

QUENQUA, DOUGLAS. "Microplastics Find Their Way Into Your Gut, a Pilot
Study Finds." *The New York Times*, 22 Oct. 2018, https://www.nytimes
.com/2018/10/22/health/microplastics-human-stool.html.

RICH, MOTOKO. "Cleansing Plastic From Oceans: Big Ask for a Country That
Loves Wrap." *The New York Times*, 27 June 2019, https://www.nytimes
.com/2019/06/27/world/asia/japan-g20-plastics-pollution.html.

ROSENTHAL, ELISABETH. "Is It Time to Bag the Plastic?" *The New York
Times*, 18 May 2013, https://www.nytimes.com/2013/05/19/sunday-review
/should-america-bag-the-plastic-bag.html.

SCHMIDT, WILLIAM E. "Local Laws Take Aim at Indestructible Trash." *The
New York Times*, 23 Apr. 1989, https://www.nytimes.com/1989/04/23
/weekinreview/the-nation-local-laws-take-aim-at-indestructible-trash
.html.

STACK, LIAM. "Ocean-Clogging Microplastics Also Pollute the Air, Study
Finds." *The New York Times*, 18 Apr. 2019, https://www.nytimes.com
/2019/04/18/science/what-are-microplastics.html.

STEVENS, WILLIAM K. "Degradable Plastics Show Promise in Fight Against Trash." *The New York Times*, 11 Apr. 1989, https://www.nytimes.com /1989/04/11/science/degradable-plastics-show-promise-in-fight-against -trash.html.

WASSENER, BETTINA. "Raising Awareness of Plastic Waste." *The New York Times*, 14 Aug. 2011, https://www.nytimes.com/2011/08/15/business /energy-environment/raising-awareness-of-plastic-waste.html.

WEINTRAUB, KAREN. "Just a Few Pieces of Plastic Can Kill Sea Turtles." *The New York Times*, 13 Sept. 2018, https://www.nytimes.com/2018/09/13 /science/sea-turtles-plastic.html.

WICHTER, ZACH. "Tackling the Plastic Problem, One City (or Country) at a Time." *The New York Times*, 22 Apr. 2019, https://www.nytimes.com/2019 /04/22/travel/tackling-the-plastic-problem-one-city-or-country-at-a-time .html.

WILSON, F. PERRY. "No Road Back to Natural Materials." *The New York Times*, 30 Mar. 1975, https://www.nytimes.com/1975/03/30/archives/no-road -back-to-natural-materials.html.

YAEGER, LYNN. "Plastic Surge." *The New York Times*, 26 Aug. 2007, https:// www.nytimes.com/2007/08/26/style/tmagazine/26plastic.html.

YAFFE-BELLANY, DAVID. "Would You Drink Water Out of a Can? Pepsi Wants to Find Out." *The New York Times*, 27 June 2019, https://www.nytimes .com/2019/06/27/business/pepsi-aquafina-water-cans.html.

YEGINSU, CEYLAN. "European Parliament Approves Ban on Single-Use Plastics." *The New York Times*, 25 Oct. 2018, https://www.nytimes.com /2018/10/25/world/europe/european-parliament-plastic-ban.html.

ZHONG, RAYMOND, AND CAROLYN ZHANG. "Food Delivery Apps Are Drowning China in Plastic." *The New York Times*, 28 May 2019, https://www.nytimes .com/2019/05/28/technology/china-food-delivery-trash.html.

Index

This book is current up until the time of printing. For the most up-to-date reporting, visit www.nytimes.com.